Part-Time Angels

Part-Time Angels

... and 75 Others

RICHARD BACH

ISBN-13: 978-1514385562
ISBN-10: 1514385562

10 9 8 7 6 5 4 3 2 1

Contents

Introduction

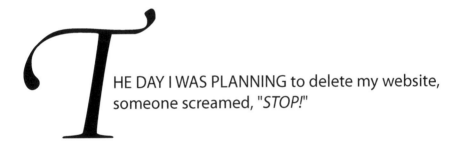HE DAY I WAS PLANNING to delete my website, someone screamed, "*STOP!*"

She got my attention. So startling the voice was, that I said, "What?"

And when she knew I was not going to light the fire that sudden astonished instant, she calmed, and said, "Are you sure you want to delete the website, all these stories?"

"Yes, that's true." My heart started beating again. "I know that."

"These are your own sheep," she said, "and you're destroying them? And you don't care?"

"They're not sheep, they're words. They've been read. So I'll just sweep the ashes, make room for other words."

"*Whisk?* All gone?"

"That's what I'm planning. Do you mind?"

"OK. They might as well be buried. I'm sorry I screamed."

"What do you mean, they might as well be buried?"

"They're lovely stories, but if someone wanted to read them all on the Internet, they had to spend hours bringing up old ones. Today, since the someone is comfortable, knows how easy it is find things in books, they'll never . . ."

"You think they're lovely?"

"Why yes, I do. You talk about being lonely, so your readers might think . . ."

"Writers talk about all sorts of things that happen to them. I never wrote a word about murders or wars or accidents, though, at least not much. I don't do that."

"But you know that people usually kill themselves when they're lonely. Mostly men, more than women, but even so some things hint that you're lonely."

"Well, I'm not lonely now!"

"Anybody reading the book will think you are."

"The book? What book?"

"Silly mortal! When you take the stories and put them on paper, it's called a 'book.'"

"I wasn't going to print any book."

"You weren't going to print the book. You are now. True or false?"

"You think they'll be a book, the collection of them?"

"Yes."

"Maybe nobody will read them."

"Maybe they won't. It isn't a writer's job to sell books."

"And my job is just to write pages of . . ."

". . . everything that's a joy to you. Yes, that's your job."

"What if nobody pays me?"

"Too bad. You don't get paid."

"But if I write this book, someone could pay me, just a little, if they wanted to?"

"That's the way it works. You know that. Four of your boo . . ."

"Five of them. Bestsellers, you mean? Five of them."

"But the rest of them, they didn't . . ."

"*Do not dare say that!* I love my books! Why, I think the ferret stories . . ."

". . . they're brilliant. The best writing you've ever put on paper. Maybe you wrote them just for a little family of readers, now, a whole little nation of them."

"That's kind of you. Just for a small family. I like that idea."

"Same with this collection of bright little sheep."

"Just for a small family? Yes. You know, just because the family is small does not mean that the writing doesn't matter to them. Even if I say I'm lonely, which I used to be."

"But not now. You can say that in the introduction. You were lonely but you're not lonely now. It's a mortal's life, sometimes to be lonely."

"Not now. But when I was, I had my times to be lonely."

"Gone in a flash, by the way. A whole mortal life is just a flash. Don't get me started about never-endings and space-time, all right? That's not why I'm here."

"Oh? Why are you here?

"Simple job. Just to keep you from destroying the stories."

"And soon as I promise, you'll be gone."

"Could be."

"I promise."

What do you think, dear reader?

Of course. The second I promised, I never heard from that sweet little angel again.

— Richard Bach
May, 2015

*W*hen We Don't Like the World

*W*RITERS ARE CONTROL freaks. It isn't that we want to have some things happen as we wish in our own lives, it's that we want everything and everyone to do exactly as we want them to do.

Writers want the stars to change, the weather to shift, the geography, the wild animals, tame ones too, countries, politics, every person, all destinies, every relationship, every thought . . . every dream needs to be just as we decide it shall be.

I didn't know this until this morning. I didn't realize that if there's anything I don't like in the world, I erase it.

The media, for instance, they chat about the few things they believe which will sell (they call it "News"), and whole cultures are bent to believe what's reported is true.

Reporters, for instance, believe that sharks are thoughtless destroyers of the sea, and reading, we think that must be true, no matter the tens of millions of sharks that don't much mind about humans nearby.

Or they believe that the twin towers collapsed a hundred floors, suddenly collapsed into their footprint because an airplane apparently hit them, and that a building nearby collapsed even without even a single touch from an airplane. It took me forever, to believe the buildings were deliberately demolished.

Because I had chosen to be a writer, and because I am a control freak, the day after September 11 was easy: I removed the television set from my house. Why should I see that piece of film another 20,000 times again? Because the media thought I'd be hypnotized to see it?

What a wonder! Television gone, no more commentators, no more film, no more beliefs of a hateful world, no more advertisers who agree what I should think and buy, never a vote from me to destroy whatever our politics and media wanted to destroy.

So of course I had to build a different world, easy enough, given the invention of the pencil and paper / the typewriter / the word-processing computer.

I removed most humans from a world of ferrets, wrote ferret

astronomy, their geography, their weather; the animals were all of them seen from a ferret's life, from their point of view. All of a sudden I was the loving media of The Ferret Chronicles.

What did I so dislike of the human world, left out to be trashed with the television set? On my delete-list were the ideas of wars, of crime, of victims, of hatred, of evil, of mortals' fascination with killing others. Take all of those, wrap them in a magic tablecloth, and—pouf!—they don't exist! Not for me, not for my books.

Ferrets are bright little animals to humans: graceful, quick, thoughtful, beautiful, they're curious, they love action, they have a sudden sense of humor. *They* could be my world!

So five books were written (and one other, a collection that was all of the five combined).

Ferrets, without the bizarre human-driven failings, raised their kits with respect always, urged them to follow their highest right, to live the adventures they imagined.
There could have been dozens of the books, but the sales weren't there, the books stopped at five. The last book was a paperback since the publisher decided to cut its hardcover losses.

But those five include the very best writing I've done, there was not a single Bad Guy in the series, and I hoped the books might be ones a young person could read to their parents. I loved the world of the ferrets, and so did some of the readers.

For me, the control-freak, there were storms and angel-ferret-fairies and subtle destinies for the ones who lived on the page. And one day I realized the bizarre truth . . . I preferred to live in the ferret world, not the human one.

We could change the human world, bit by bit, reader by reader, I thought. We could read the Courtesies of the ferrets, and to know that each reader didn't need the human world to change, they could simply begin living now, to their own highest principles.

The one thing that we control freaks don't often do, is to force our stories on readers. So today, unforced, there are just a few copies of the ferret books around the world, published in many languages.

There's a full set of the series in English on my bookshelf, and on that shelf is my world. The stars, the storms, the striving to bring ideals into every-day life: here they are.

Maybe I haven't transfigured the world of mortals, with my

control freakishness, but I changed my own little world, and perhaps the worlds of a rare few readers, too, the ones who finish these rare books with a smile.

*P*art-Time Angels

*H*OW MANY TIMES, in your life, have you done something nice for other people? Something thoughtful? How many smiles have you spent for them? How many puppies and kittens have you petted? How often, when someone is thinking of killing themselves, have you said, "I think your idea's a permanent fix for a temporary problem."

In all of those times (which you have mostly forgotten), in every one, you have been an angel.

In the midst of 1961, on a Manhattan sidewalk, an attractive woman looked at me, and in passing on the stream of other-bound pedestrians, she smiled at me for a second. I don't know why: maybe she was just happy. But that was (2015 − 1961 =) 54 years ago, and I still smile back to her, whether she's somewhere in New York, in some other country, whether she's on this planet or not.

She was an angel, changing my life in one second. Just yesterday I had a message from a friend who was standing in a troubled checkout line, everyone there was wanting to get this shopping finished and someone was slowing the line. She said, "Maybe we're being slowed up here because a car's going to kill us if we move ..." Everyone laughed, and the next minute a car drove half-way through the window of the market. No one was hurt.

Someone remembered her words, to a reporter, and the newspaper next day said that there was an angel there, who made us all stop, and saved our lives for not being in front of that window at that moment.

My friend said, "I'm no angel! I just thought of some funny reason for us to stay where we were." Do you think she was no angel? If not, I'll give her fifty angel-points for her smile and for thinking to say what she said when she did.

When we consider the millions of kind and thoughtful deeds others do for others and for us, and which we do for them, of course we realize that there's a need for us amateurs to be temporary angels.

How will that feel, to be given angel-points some day, from a full-time angel?

The Beautiful F-86F, and for Some Reason, Not Dying

I'VE BEEN WORKING a bit, flying and making some of Puff's details a little bit righter. I work in a quiet hangar, and I'm used to the tests I'm given. I'll drop a bolt and it takes two minutes to get it again, I need a tool and it takes minutes to find it, everything takes a lot of time just to do the simplest tasks.

But I'm happy with that, and the time is well spent. I knew, many years ago, that some day I'd be reading many books and learning much about death and dying, and when I'm not fastening some part of the airplane or greasing fittings or setting a new instrument in place, that's what I've been studying.

Answers About the Afterlife, by Bob Olson, seems mostly the way things are, according to my own inner truth-meter. In Michael Newton's book *The Destiny of Souls*, there's even a diagram of a meeting-room I entered when I had a near-death event in Argentina. It was startling, since I had that experience before the book was written, and here it was, a drawing of the curved desk, the elders, me, my spirit guide behind me on the left . . . on page 206. It didn't mention the elders could laugh at me.

I realized in time that "death" is a term coined by very young souls. Shifting into our next world was too much for them. Wiser ones could have termed it "Life." Those who have been there, say it's brighter, more colorful, we move instantly from one belief of a site to another, there is no judgment, no punishment unless we prefer to live a life that will give us the feelings we gave to others, which many of us do.

While I was tightening bolts in the landing gear, a simple two-minute job that took me 20 minutes, I was thinking about dying, back to the moment when I very nearly flew into the ground. All the feelings are still there, and I lived them once again, fifty-eight years later.

The airplane was a North American F-86F *Sabre*: single engine, single seat, and for its time it was very fast. It's easy to think about, since it is one of the two most beautiful aircraft ever designed (the other is the Supermarine Spitfire).

I was training on a gunnery range, which existed since there were no computers to simulate the practice. There were three of us that day, who were learning how to shoot. They had told us the day before, "You'll want to be careful, gentlemen. Target fixation will kill you. We lost an airplane yesterday that way, he flew into the target. If your pass isn't working, don't try to make it better. You're going too fast to watch your burst and correct it. Just pull up early and try it again."

It was easy to say Yes, sir.

The things that have haunted me all my life were these:

It was a cold morning in the desert south of Phoenix, Arizona, January, 1958. The four of us were to take off at 0700.

My position was Number Two in a four-ship formation, I was wingman of the instructor's airplane.

The weather was fine: cold, but no clouds.

Like the other students, I had memorized what was to happen. We'd fly a square pattern around the Applied Tactics range, which was old trucks and tanks parked in the desert), and today we'd load all six machine guns in the '86.

Till then we had only loaded two guns. This time we were going to feel what it was like to be in a combat situation. We'd keep our hands on the windscreen before takeoff, so the armorers knew we weren't going to pull the trigger while they armed the guns. When they were finished, they'd slap the nose of the airplane, and the guns would be ready to fire.

An easy flight to the range, a nice low pass and the leader pulled up into the range pattern, I counted one, two, THREE! and pulled up to follow him.

Set the switches to make the guns hot, my finger not touching the trigger on the control stick.

Then the leader called "Champagne's in and hot," and started his gunnery pass. I was next.

"Two's in and hot." That was me. Watch the airspeed as I slanted down. Three hundred fifty knots for the pass. The gunsight was a bright pattern, a circle of diamonds, the pipper was a little white ball in the center, the image where the bullets would converge.

There were the targets, coming up, coming up, and I touched the trigger when the diamonds circled a truck. The first movement of the trigger started the gun camera, the second was the muffled sound of the machine guns. They seemed faraway, distant. I smelled the gunpowder in the cockpit, and the airplane slowed from the recoil of the six guns. The truck flashed beneath me, gone in a second.

I pulled up for the next pass. I couldn't tell if I had hit anything, the bullets were striking as I pulled up.

"Three's in and hot." A nice pattern. Not what it would be if we were ever going to use the airplane in combat, the patterns would come from different directions.

My turn again. "Two's in and hot." Wish I could see the bullets. How do I know if I hit the target when I can't see my burst?

Three hundred fifty knots. There was the little truck under my gunsight. Right about NOW, the guns were popcorn, harmless. I held the trigger and there, I could see the ground coming apart to the left of the truck, looking close now. I banked a tiny bit to the right, and all of a sudden I could see there were little flowers on the sagebrush. The door on the truck was hanging loose and rusted untouched by my flying, though they might not be after the rest of the bullets rained down.

That's when I knew I was dead. The ground was directly in front of me, suddenly huge. I knew I had done the same thing that the pilot yesterday had done. He had seen his own bullets hit the target.

The impulse to snatch the control stick was in my wrist. It could take a hundredth of a second to effect the controls. Way too late.

Everything went black. No gift of death, but of a huge updraft directly beneath the airplane. The G force snapped my head down and I saw nothing. By the time I could see, a couple seconds later, the F-86 was several hundred feet above the ground, the impulse in my wrist had pulled the stick back and we were flying.

I heard a voice, the first one I had ever heard, not someone on the radio, not someone in the airplane:

"The hand of God."

I checked the recording accelerometer, it was well above 8 G's, well over the maximum G for the airplane. I no longer cared about shooting, that day. I called for the leader:

"Champagne, it's Two. I've overstressed the aircraft."

A brief silence. "You WHAT!"

In a few seconds he was flying alongside of my airplane, sliding below me, looking for panels missing. "Let's go home. SFO. Fly it easy. Three, you're leader, finish the mission."

— *Gene I. Dexter*

A simulated flame-out pattern is a big lazy circle to land. My '86 lowered her wheels when I asked her to, landed with no difficulty. Guns unloaded, taxied to the ramp, shut down the engine. When the crew chief came up the ladder, I told him what had happened. He frowned, nodded, went down to the ground, began looking for failed rivets. I don't know whether he found them or not.

So here I am today, working on Puff, asking the same questions, getting no answers.

Why wasn't I killed in the desert? Other pilots told me it was an updraft, that saved me.

But the morning was cold, there are no updrafts in icy mornings. Let alone updrafts at that precise instant, and with enough force . . .

I figured it out. An airspeed of 350 knots, going down, in an airplane that weighed 15,000 pounds, it would have needed a updraft of at least 120,000 pounds, sixty tons fired upward, at the instant I happened to be there, in that calm air, so close to the ground—that is not possible.

The hand of God? Poetic, and I didn't disagree. But the physics . . . it isn't possible.

Yet here I am, in the belief of here and now, working on Puff's landing gear. Another voice saved me years later than the desert God. Are there angels, is there something that keeps me from dying? That bet I plan to win, for the fun of discovering—rediscovering, death. I guess they decided not to call it Life, since everyone would have rushed there forgetting they had tests to meet in this lifetime. But it's true. Has my amnesia worn off? Am I homesick for Life again?

Puff thinks not. She rarely talks when her engine is stopped, but it sounded like her. How can you be homesick, when our home is with our spirit, every minute?

She had died in the crash two years ago, she had been pure spirit till we finally rebuilt her body.

I know that's true, what she said. Our home is now, forever. Yet it's my test. I've got to prove it, before long.

A Story with Puff

TODAY WAS THE DAY I finished most of the maintenance for Puff, and it was time to fly.

I pulled her out of her hangar, looked over all the nuts and bolts, the tension on the cables, made sure that all the hinges were working smoothly, the flight controls, added some fuel and oil for the flight. It had been several weeks since I had landed in the water, for all this maintenance, and I was just a little nervous as I slid into the cockpit, fastened the seat belt and shoulder harness, started the engine. This flight would take us to the lake again.

More than any airplane I've owned, Puff had somehow learned to talk with me (and I had learned how to talk with her), and we flew thousands of miles, happily chatting about the events of our flights. I don't know if you remember, but after our crash with the high-tension wires, Puff had been silent.

When I could walk again, I had some talks with her spirit (her body, wings and tail were destroyed, waiting in pieces on the floor of the hangar), and she told me that when I rebuilt her body it would be a little confused, and would not talk much.

It was true. My friend Dan Nickens offered his own airplane's spare wings and tail, a gift from his Jenn to Puff, her sister ship. When she was finished and ready to fly again, she flew perfectly. And sure enough, she didn't speak. For five flights, silence. Then suddenly she said, "Hi," as we climbed up from a lake, in Florida, and she was quiet again.

Flying her from Florida to Washington State was a delight for Dan once again. We flew her after she arrived home, some land landings, some water landings so I was at least capable again of flying her after a long time on the ground. Dan left her with me, took a commercial airline home.

That's the story till the engine-start today: Puff had become silent in the air, on the ground. She was a wonderful airplane, but she wasn't talking. Not a word while I worked on her. Not a word now, her engine running, warming.

At noon we took off, toward a lake on the mainland—I wanted her first flights today to be in fresh water.

It would take half an hour to get to the lake from the island. I settled down thinking about the landings. Triple check the wheels UP, Richard, for a water landing. At 60 mph lower the flaps, slow down, snuggle down to the water, keep the nose a little up . . .

It was not just me, I thought. There were two of us. I said old habit, "Are you ready Puff? Water landings today."

I expected silence.

"I'll be fine," I heard her in my mind.

I blinked, then answered. "You've had some difficult times, Puff, the last years."

"So did you," she said.

I had to laugh. Yes, I've had some difficult times, too. I said it again. "Are you ready to fly, Puff? We're heading to the lake."

She sang. "We're goin' to the water; We're goin' to splash in the blue!"

I couldn't believe it. Puff was singing to me! A funny little song, made me dissolve my tension, made me laugh again.

What happened to the silent cockpit?   Puff was funny, up-beat. As though she wanted me to feel happy, too.

We talked for the next ten minutes, all of it bright and happy, more of her singing and talking, than me. She made it part of her song, that she was flying again, and she was home and she was glad to be in the air again with me.

We skirted a mountain and there was the lake. A gentle

breeze, little wavelets on the surface.

I checked the gear.

"My wheels are folded up," she sang. "they're all tucked away . . ."

Slowed to 60, lowered the flaps,

". . . and down come the flaps, like little mice, down, down . . ."

Careful, Richard, I thought. Close to the water. Closer Gentle . . . now, hold her off . . .

"Like a little dandelion, we're going to gently gently touch . . ."

And that moment I heard her hull clipping the tops of the wavelets and then slowing, squinching into the water.

"Hmm . . . hmm . . . hm . . . hm . . . We're splashing in the water, splashing like moonlight . . ."

When she's nearly stopped, some of the water flew from the spray into the cockpit

". . . and my pilot's getting wet . . ."

It was a perfect landing. Truly, it was perfect. Puff was silent for a second. "See? You can land as well as you ever did!"

It felt terrific, the cold water getting warm on my life preserver.

Then throttle up, her engine spinning top speed, Puff lifted light in the water, just skimming, white feathers of her spray way behind us; and she was in the air.

"Oh, somebody loves the water," she sang, "I wonder who . . ."

The second landing, same thing . . . perfect. And the third, again . . . perfect.

As though she were landing herself.

". . . and my pilot's the best pilot, in the whole wooorld . . ."

We did some step taxiing, 30 mph, trailing spray the way I once trailed contrails at high altitude, long ago.

Then off again, up again and home. Over the water we flew a foot or two over the sea, a sailboat in the sky.

Puff was silent once again. Then, "You're feeling good?"

"Puff, you know that. You fly so sweetly, your little dance, mid-air."

"It's our dance."

Then we landed on the runway, taxied to the hangar, and she didn't say a word.

Soon as I got home, I emailed Dan Nickens. "Got the service list done for Puff, and today, with a 5 knot wind, I went out for some water exercise.

"On the way to the lake, Dan, ten, fifteen minutes after takeoff, Puff started talking! I think it was her, but different from at first and different from after the rebuilding, when she was so silent. She was bright and happy and funny! Never seen that before. I was letting down for the water, checking the gear up, the flaps for the first time in the water. And she was singing! The first landing was perfect. Then off again two more times and some step turns. All of them, everything was perfect . . ."

He wrote back at once:

"YES! She's BACK!

"Well, she never left, but now she's really back with us in this space-time. That is so good for you, her, and all of us, Puff's fans.

"Her quietness . . . . . . Could it be that she was checking your sincerity . . . your commitment? I don't know how she could doubt it. You did show it by caring for her over the past weeks.

"You've probably read of the cases: trauma renders a person mute. Unwilling or unable to face what happened, they withdraw into themselves. They just don't want to have to deal with this reality.

"Until . . .

"Until they are drawn back by someone who loves them.

"Could that be Puff? So suddenly to jump back into this game? And to land here with such aplomb? Ta-Dah?

"Or has she just been waiting. Waiting for the two of you to need to be better than the one?

"No, I don't know. But you do, or will.

"What I do know is that I couldn't be happier for you or Puff. Perfect together again."

—*Dan Nickens*

The Leaf Who Touched Madrid

IT HAPPENED THREE YEARS ago, in October. I was walking with Zsa-Zsa, or rather I was walking down a grassy road on the property and she was being a Shetland sheepdog exploring the lefts and rights of the road, checking to make sure the squirrels were properly where they belonged, in the trees instead of on the ground, that the sparrows were in the sky and not resting on the grass, that all the mice had their little passports to travel the covered mini-roads over the meadow.

Winter would be here, and ZZ would soon have to taste the snowflakes, check out the footprints of raccoons, watch eagles shake their frost and fly from the tallest trees.

There was a grand maple tree along the road, and my boots crunched a thousand leaves on the ground. The leaves on the tree were dying, too. Seasons, I thought, they bring gentle deaths to so much of nature, and they ready our days for new life, too.

The next step, I stopped. For there on the road among all the dead leaves was a leaf that was perfectly green, a song of summer past. I picked it up, and the one next to it. I could hardly believe, so I took my little phone-camera and took a picture.

(This is not a color book. Please imagine the leaf on the left is bright green, the one to its right is a dry brown, crunchy.)

How strange! Every other leaf, every one on the ground, was dried and brown. The one, as though it was linked ever to eternal life, glowed in the road.

What a remarkable sight. I put it down again, and continued my walk with Zsa-Zsa. She was out of sight, but of course she knew exactly where I was. How did that leaf stay so green?

I wandered in the forest, but I couldn't get the leaf out of my mind. There must be some reason . . . I never much cared for biology, I didn't know what had happened to this leaf. I must have thought it was green, a few minutes ago. I didn't imagine it green, did I? Finally I turned home again, hiked back up the road, found the tree, saw the leaf. The same leaf. I picked it up from the road, brought it home, protected it from ZZ, who wanted to inspect it carefully.

I put the two leaves on the table. They stayed there. Months later, the snow swirling, drifting out the window, the leaf stayed, untouched by dogs or nature. In time, it began to dry. I picked it up, and part of the leaf shattered, fell to the floor.

Something happened somehow, a sheepdog may have gotten onto the table and curious, touched it with a paw, when it fractured into a hundred pieces.

Still, I had made another photograph:

Then today, I had an email from Madrid, from a friend at the website. She had been healed miraculously, she thought, and she had read The *Biology of Belief* by Bruce Lipton. I thought to tell her about the leaf, and she wrote back:

"Wow! The leaf! I thought that only happened to human beings! They say that happens to humans whose vibrations are really high, their bodies remain intact for a long time when they die, it seems their cells are impregnated with their high vibrations! I never thought it could happen to leaves, too! Is it possible that this was a leaf whose life was dedicated to Love? Can Love alter the cycle of Mortal Life? Can Love affect atoms and cells in such a way that in ecstasies they forget what they have to do when they die? That time stops for them and they remain as they are? Are you aware of the little miracle you kept at home?

"And you say you are not fascinated by Biology! In what way can vibrations of a leaf be that high? Maybe, aware of danger, she bent one day to save the life of a little caterpillar. I have heard that plants suffer fear, or experience joy. They are sensitive to all the emotions around them, you can register fear with electrodes when you approach them with a sharp object. If they can feel fear, can they feel Love? Was your leaf a loving one?

"It is amazing. How lucky you are! How lucky she is! She fell just where you would find her, you, the one being who would notice, so her loving life did not disappear into oblivion. The vibrations of those beings are so high that they affect also those of the ones around them, maybe your little leaf can help you raise your own awareness. Wait a minute! Isn't she doing it just know? Yours and mine?"

I wrote back: "I walk by that tree. This year, not a single green leaf remains! Lots and lots, seas of brown leaves. I can only agree with you, that it was that leaf's love, her bending to save the life of a caterpillar that let the love of the Universe ripple through all the beliefs of dying.

"Look at what she's done to thee and me: Never will we forget her, the wonder of her life will continue through us, and some day through your daughters, and through those to whom we share her story. She is invisible to us today, sparkling among all the stars, like *The Little Prince's* Asteroid B-612, living her life in the spirit of all the leaves that ever lived. Some day, or perhaps for many days to come, we will scuff through the fallen leaves, and know that she floats perfect always, right now, this minute."

And today, at last, the leaf shifts into your consciousness.

Happy summer!

*I*t's 2:00 AM

N A TUESDAY.

I am wide awake.

The little Shelty puppy will be off on his flight to Washington in three hours.

He is already immortal, already a perfect expression of perfect Love, as are we, too. He is already beautiful in the timeless spaceless realm of Here and Now. He will arrive here (by my own belief), in a few hours, when we've agreed to begin a little adventure in our fantasy of space and time.

He can sleep for this flight. He has his own spirit guides with him now, floating near him. He is perfect as the guides are perfect. So am I. So are we all, untouched by the pretend world that once appeared so large and powerful.

No matter what seems to be, our perfection is already and forever true.

We have met before on Earth, the puppy and us, too, and we will meet again. I am grateful, deeply grateful, for this beautiful event. And for the many others which have guided us, year after year on year.

The death of Lucky, the crash, this belief of this very moment, is every one part of the story we've been blessed to have written.

So many stories! So bright the colors we're writing!

*G*uess What?

HE'S HERE AT LAST, in my home—his home. At the moment, he's curled up by my side as I write (my right hand moving slowly, not to disturb him), and he's sound asleep.

How ideas take form. Not just form, but sometimes personalities, close to our hearts.

A few weeks ago, I never once thought of getting a Sheltie puppy. Then came the memory of my dear Lucky in old communication, and all of a sudden I was living a sequence of moments that he said would happen. Soon as it happened, I could look for him here in our belief of spacetime!

Then everything stopped, I looked everywhere, found no dog, no nothing, finally a photo of a remarkably similar

Sheltie puppy, so familiar. I bought him. He arrived by airline yesterday, in fine shape.

He is calm and thoughtful. Strange, for a puppy, normal for Lucky.

He was instantly comfortable with me. As was I with him.

He barks rarely, un-Sheltie-like. But Lucky rarely barked.

He puts his chin on my wrist, looks as me sideways when I talk. As Lucky did.

He walks with me, no leash required, from the first day. He remembers?

Does this puppy carry the same sense as the one I loved years before? He seems to have that way about him, so far.

This puppy has needle-teeth, same as Lucky had, of course, when he was a puppy. Both of them could have bit hard, neither of them did, nor do. Light enough to say, "*I have powerful teeth, but I'm only biting you at about 18 percent of my full bite. I don't want to hurt you.*"

Is he the same personality, is this puppy a re-born Lucky? Is anything different?

The markings between the two, that's different, and a subtle sense of change. The Lucky I remember is not a puppy, this one is. Is that the change?

I'm coming to think that each of us has a one-time personality, no two aspects of us exactly identical across lifetimes, and each of the other choices has a subtly different personality.

Someone very much like my old Sheltie, but a little different. As I would be different, if I chose to be re-born. Do each of us have a one-time stamp of personality, unique, somehow, from all the others? My guess, based on this puppy—yes.

For the last couple of weeks, the little guy has changed. Lucky's comment three years ago after he died: "If ever a person walks through the door and talks about Shetland Sheepdogs. I'll be there. You'll find me in the south of this property."

Not a single Sheltie here today in Seattle, in Washington; not puppies, adults, shelter guests, not one of the breed available;

But one in Missouri, south of here by 1,500 miles, one single photograph I found in a host of other cute puppies which did not call to me;

Yet this one puppy, his expression at the second the camera clicked looked exactly like Lucky's;

He was available to me when he could have been sold instantly.

Between the time I saw his photos and the time he arrived in Washington, there were an uncountable number of mistakes that could have happened. Weather delays, maintenance delays, a baggage error, a hijacking . . . not one of them happened.

He arrived at the cargo port, the place where Steve Roos at Delta Airlines had read many of my books. Very rare, but fun,

I was glad to hear that, and Steve told me the minute the puppy arrived . . . not a second's delay;

After a nine hour road-and-flight from St. Louis to Salt Lake City to Seattle, and a five-hour drive home, he was one bright puppy.

He is still that way. Everything was in order for him, all the details were perfect.

His name? Not quite the same as it was: *Lockie*, ". . . a pet name for the Scottish Lachian," according to the Wikipedia. Interesting—"a pet name." Pronounced the same, but subtlety different.

One of the differences is that he doesn't come to the call of "Lockie!" But he does look sideways at it.

Time, and Answers

WE BEGIN, as mortals on Earth, with a million questions.

By the time we're four or five years into our beliefs here, we know there are answers and we intend to find them. And sure enough, by the time we've spent a few decades here, watched blessings that we thought were disasters when they happened, we have some answers that work for us.

Comes a time when we have so many answers that there's hardly a question we haven't resolved and we sail easily through the deep waters that once were reefs and shoals of unsolved mysteries.

Troubles are events for us, we don't have to worry about what used to be the tests, to be the problems for us to solve. By the time difficult times arrive, we've already got matched answers trotting four abreast.

But all these answers! Can we share them with those few who might be interested?

Can we list a problem that seemed to be impossible when we met it, and that's now a quiet gentle answer?

I don't know, but I'll try:

My daughter was a beautiful teenager. Years ago, there was an accident on a snowy windy night, another car left its lane and hit her automobile in a head-on collision. Minutes before, for no reason, my daughter had unfastened her seat belt. With the crash, she was killed almost instantly.

What were the odds, that two women in the other car would lose control in the snow and the wind and the dark at just the second that my daughter's car was traveling straight and level in the other lane? Every other person survived the crash.

So rare, the odds, that there was no chance of it happening. One in millions of possibilities . . . what could have told her to unlatch her seat belt and shoulder harness, at exactly the moment she did?

Is there any way to explain this thing we called a winter accident? I thought no, there's no possibility.

Not long after the crash though, my other daughter, her dearest friend, began receiving messages from her sister. She told us that her sister is happy and busy in her afterlife, that she loves being a help to young girls who have come over swiftly, who might be puzzled about what has happened and what lessons it offered for her friends and family.

How could she have understood the mission that she chose, I thought, if she had not died as she did, in the snow and the wind and the night? Had she lived a long uneventful life, could she have felt the way other young women feel, ending a lifetime early?

This story may mean nothing to some readers. Others will find a different explanation for the event: it was not a choice that we can make; it was God's will; it was bad luck.

And yet, for me, and I think for my daughters, their answer changes the shadows that darkened that night. Their answer brought light, just as we hoped it could bring, to every one of our lives.

*D*esigning A Future

ONCE UPON A TIME, I knew that our imagination was fiction, and our daily lives were fact.

Aren't there rules? Can't we write a story that seems to have happened (but didn't), and yet remember some startling event that no one believes is true (but it happened)?

Answer: No rules. All our lives are gently stirred, our recollections and our imaginations become, to the best of our knowledge, the lives we live, day after day.

Of course we can play with rules that aren't. I remember flying formation long ago, through clouds that were so dense that I could only see just the wingtip of the flight leader, the rest was fog. I had to fly breathtakingly close to his wing or he would be gone in the clouds.

Later, on the ground, and with years after the flight, I couldn't believe that clouds could so tightly packed with mist. I must have imagined that flight, I thought, and soon as I did, it became unreal. I hadn't had such a day ever, before that day, never had one after . . . it couldn't have happened, just some light mist, I'm sure. It couldn't have been. So today, it's fiction, until perhaps some reader can tell me it happened to her or to him, too. Some clouds are really dense! Then it will come back into living experience for me, once again.

I wrote a little book called *Rescue Ferrets at Sea*. A book from a few years ago, and since I loved the ferrets I decided to make them a little more true for myself and for readers.

I made a fifteen-inch insignia of the Ferret Rescue Service. Since it was to be used in rescue events with one rescue boat, I centered the FRS insignia on one boat's colors: striped orange and yellow. Other rescue boats had their own colors, but Bethany Ferret and her crew had rebuilt a wrecked boat, the *J-101 Resolute*, so if she was to have an aerial seaplane to help her rescue small mammals, the seaplane needed the *Resolute's* colors.

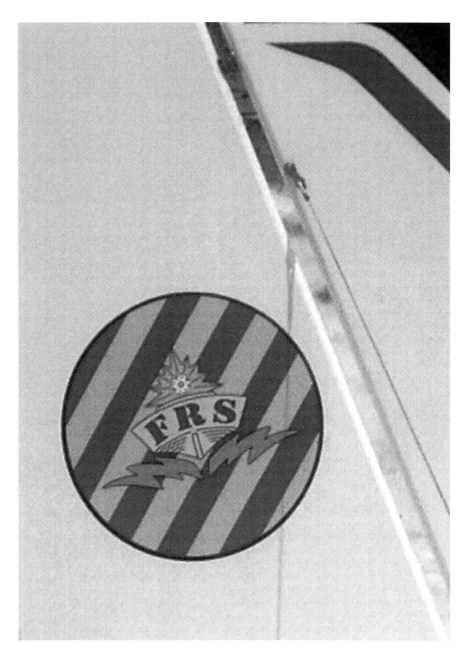

I took the insignia for the Ferret Rescue Service, took it to an embroidery shop, made a flight jacket patch for the RFS:

I guess you know what seaplane was going to fly with the FRS. Not from the pages of the book, but from the pages of my mind.

— *Dan Nickens*

Is this fiction, or is it part of the every day experience of those who happen to see the FRS aircraft fly?

And sure enough, there came to be another plane, with a pilot who flew to the water and removed a rope that could have tangled in the legs of a small mammal, and Dan Nickens and his seaplane became the second aircraft of the Ferret Rescue Service.

So there in a minute you have the story.

One time not so long ago I believed that Lucky, my dear friend and Shetland Sheepdog might be returning to earth after three years (human time) gone. I found one single Sheltie that seemed to have Lucky's characteristics. The little one, Lockie, I just discovered, was so reluctant to having a leash connected to his collar, (though he'd walk fine if Sabryna were with him) but he simply refused to walk with me. It took a hundred treats to get him to come 200 yards down the road.

At last I took the leash off, and like magic, like Lucky, he immediately walked near me wherever I wished. Little Lockie, preferred not to be forced, even if it was in the interest of his safety. I have to admit that Lucky and I feel the same way. Please don't save me from my own decisions. Even if I'll crash, some day, don't protect me from myself.

Not long ago, he was just an idea. He's a little puppy now. Lucky loved my shoes when he was a puppy, Little Lockie does, too:

Is Lockie fiction? Am I? Is our whole world, our beliefs and hopes and imagination, is that the shifting fantasy that we take for true?

For the few years of our mortal lives, maybe so.

*M*arriage of a Different Culture

I GUESS SOMETHING I had said about loneliness reached my guardian angel. She's beautiful, of course, as all of us are in our highest realms of spirit. Spoke softly, a kind of music in her voice.

"Hallo, Richard!"

"Hello, dear spirit. You're my angel?"

She laughed. "You can say that. Most of us have specialties. Safety in airplane crashes, protection from storms on land, storms at sea, accidents on roads, in elevators ... Everything that you believe can happen in a lifetime, you have angels to help when your mission in life is not quite finished."

I knew there was more for her to say, but she didn't go on. Not Telling Everything is part of an angel's training.

"Are you going to help me," I said, "with another airplane crash?"

"I don't think you'll be having another airplane crash." She was so solemn about that, that it was my turn to laugh.

"What's your specialty? There's no elevator on the island. If you're to be company for a lonely gentleman, I'll accept your offer with thanks."

"You'll need mortals for company. I'm just a busy angel. There's more in my specialty, but we're all busy."

"Forgive me. Thank you for saying hallo. My best wishes from the humans you're helping!"

She didn't move. "You want to have someone special in your life."

"Well, yes, that's true." When there's not a soul to talk with about all one's gentle brushes with life, the funny moments of our lives . . . what would you say? I said, "How did you find that out?"

"My specialty."

"Oh." So that was her job. Four years without a loving partner in my life. Well yes, I had a beautiful non-romantic friend through the crash, she's a friend now, still it would have been so much easier if my Personal Romantic Relationship Angel had found a partner before that.

"You've been busy indeed," I said.

"There's a time, and there's a not-time. It was important for you to have a not-time. You'll understand in a while."

"Maybe there's no one in this country for me. Maybe nobody in the world, ever," I said. Lots of reasons for that: I live alone, don't meet anyone in my quiet place, soon as there's a party, I'm off the other . . .

"Would you consider," she said, "a woman from a different country? I need to know. Is someone from a different culture, would they . . . ?"

"I'd love it. I could learn a language, help teach English . . ."

"Language is easy," she said. "Would you enjoy loving with a woman from a different culture?"

I was a minute before responding. "I have a problem with religions," I said. "If the culture has parades for religious statues, of holy days that I think are lost on us, I'd have a little difficulty with that."

There was a checklist on her mind. "You don't like religions. You don't care about age?"

"Now wait. If someone's so young that she has no ideas of her own, that would never work. I'd need to find someone who knew, who had lived some tests, someone who had learned that the answers are within us, even if our spirit guides have to drag them on stage."

"Drag anyone? I don't think we've ever dragged . . . Tell me an age."

"Someone who's thought it all through . . . how can I give a number for all that experience. And young women want to have children. I don't."

"Tell me an age."

"Thirty five?" I said. "Thirty five and they probably know they have answers, and they don't need children."

"Thirty five. And the top number for an age?"

"Any number is fine."

"But you like beautiful women."

"That's important. But I know an actress," I said, "I think she's spent more time in this life than I have. She's wildly beautiful. Of course I like beauty. I don't care about counting age."

"OK, from thirty five to any age beyond."

"Yes." Click on the checklist.

"Culture?"

"There have to be Italians, the Spanish, French, German, Swedish women who aren't connected with a religion, aren't there? No problem with the culture. Of course I want one person, not families."

"Same for near eastern countries, African, Asian? Does

culture have any thing except religion that will stop you?

"I don't care for wars . . ."

She laughed. "No wars? You flew war planes!"

"I was mid-twenties the one time the United States had no wars. The Berlin Crisis, later cooled. If I were in the military at thirty five, I wouldn't choose me for a friend. I've already allowed for some learning. The trouble with the military . . ."

She frowned. "Are we discussing the military?" she said. "I thought you wanted someone to love."

"Sorry."

She smiled. "Are you old fashioned?"

"Very funny. No I don't need an open marriage. I like us to talk about decisions. No, I'm not independent. Yes, I'm old fashioned."

"Anything else?"

"Her travels are finished. She loves a country place. She plays with her imagination. Smart, of course. Loving."

She smiled. ". . . likes Shetland Sheepdogs."

I blinked.

Of course! I didn't have to say a word to this angel! "You know everything about me, don't you?"

"It's nice if you tell me, too."

"But you don't need me to say . . ." We can't hide anything, I thought. Angel guides know. A test for her: "How do I like my special love to wear her hair?'

"What do you like? Long, Straight. Dark.".

"I knew it. You already know!"

"How can I find a perfect woman for you if I didn't know?"

I looked at her for a half-minute. Everything about her was . . . "She looks like you, doesn't she?"

"It's easier when I mirror an image of her for you."

"So where is she? How to I find her?"

"Richard, there are thousands of women across the world you'll find are beautiful, have a bright sense of humor, are smart, loving, speak English, love Shelties . . . thousands!"

She was quiet. I thought it was my turn to talk. "Oh, the problem is me, isn't it?"

"Could be. They're looking for someone different from you."

"The crash?"

"For some, the crash. For others, you've been in this life too long."

That got my attention, of course. There's a time for mortals when the belief of age stops attraction. "But you're here with me now. Is it time for you to tell me that all I've done and said, you're going to say it doesn't matter? Romance dies with the belief of age? You're going to tell me I'll have to wait till my next lifetime?"

"Not really. You'll change appearance soon as you enter the belief of the afterlife."

"Oh. You're saying that I just need to die."

She looked at me, hint of a smile. "Tell me. Are you a difficult test for a mortal woman now?"

"I've loved a few women. Didn't seem hard to meet them. When you love someone, it's hard for them to be a test for you."

She looked a question at me. "Richard, you are a quiet man. You live on a little island on the very edge of the United States, on a mountain-top, in a place that very few people visit, you're surrounded by private lands, behind a gate, you go nowhere where you meet others, you don't travel, your telephone is unlisted, you have practically no mail, you almost never give interviews, your website is unknown to almost every person on the earth, your email address is just this side of secret. If you wanted to be totally unknown, Richard, tell me: what else could you do beyond what you're doing, this minute?"

A long silence. "Umm . . .   I could shut down the computer?"

"That would help." She just looked at me, the little smile, and all at once I knew how difficult her job must be. I had asked my Personal Romantic Relationship Angel to do the impossible.

"When you put it that way, I don't have a lot to say."

"Well, not to worry," she said, ready for a challenge. "There's not much for you to do in the mortal world, but there are a few things I can do. The principle of coincidence, I'll turn some wheels. Much to happen with the magnetism of like hearts. Invisible powers you can count on, when material powers are gone."

"I believe you." I said. "Invisible powers."

"We've met before.," she said. "We will again. So many lifetimes."

When she said that, I knew we needed a long talk. "I'll be gone from your eyes now," she said, "but I'll still be near." A nod of her head, a flash of her smile, and she was gone.

Not a second for me to say thank you, I didn't tell her how much she meant to me. *So many lifetimes.* Was *she* the one I so wanted to meet?

She didn't ask for thanks. All the angel spirit guides, busy beyond time, they do it for the fun of their work.

What a lovely belief for us to live!

*E*xorcism by Love

REMEMBER LOCKIE? That sweet, that dear, calm, gentle, thoughtful, wise, understanding, soft, fluffy little Shetland Sheepdog puppy who walked with me a few steps, no leash, never barked, who captivated my heart with a single look?

He was so sweet, for two days in my house. I was so kind to him! I told him that this was now his house, and the lands around, they were his lands. He was a Sheltie Prince. Because these words were in the past tense, you suspect that there was a change.

You're right.

Third day, a fine day for walking, but oddly enough, my shoes were gone! Could I have left them in the car? Why would I have done such a th . . . I took a few steps toward the car, and there they were, both of my shoes, on Lockie's little pillow-bed in my bedroom. He could barely rest there in his pillow, since the shoes were so big, the two of them. I must have left them out and this neat little Prince and Butler took them under his care.

That's fine, we'll go for a walk. A short walk, a quarter of a mile, and for the time he should wear a little harness that I'll clip to a leash.

I watched him at one end of the room, blinked for a second, and he was at the opposite end of the room . . . ZAM! I thought he was probably going to be an awfully fast runner, so wouldn't it seem reasonable to leash a puppy for his first real walk? Aren't there so many places in a forest for a new Sheltie to get lost at such high speed? I agree. Until he learns the boundaries of his home, a leash is reasonable.

So I fitted him with the Size Small harness, he seemed to enjoy it. I clipped on the leash, carried him out to the forest road, set him gently down, and said, "Good boy, Lockie, let's have a walk!"

Nothing. My runner was stone at the end of the leash. "C'mon Lockie, time for your walk!"

I tugged lightly on the leash and the dog went berserk. He tugged back so hard I lost my balance, and when I could see him again, he was a spiral-eye evil spirit at the end of the leash. He thrashed wildly, I saw a blurred vision of non-stop tumbling paw-springs, a twisting backward layout that a pit-bull couldn't survive. He was a crazed mountain colt under three lariats of *The Misfits*, Marilyn Monroe would have locked me into the lowest hell for dog-tormentors.

I ran to him, let go of the leash and fortunately caught him on the bounce, held him tightly. The leash, or was it the harness, it was the bridge of crazy spirits.

He calmed after a minute. "Lockie, it's just a leash! It's for your safety!" I set him down. He was trembling.

"It's just a little walk," I said. "Leash for your safety . . ." I had touched the handle of the leash and Lockie went into orbit fell onto his back, feet in the sky, "I'll-die-if-you-drag-me-inverted-on-the-string! Kill-me-if-you-must-I'm-only-a-little-puppy!!!"

Half a glance from Marilyn, "You *MONSTER! RICHARD I hope I NEVER see you AG . . .*" and I was done.

"No walk, Lockie. No leash, no harness, no nothing!" He trembled till he was free, in the house again.

I called my friend Sabryna. "You know the puppy? Lockie? The same one we drove home from the airport?"

"Of course."

"Evil spirits!"

She heard my story, wasn't frightened. "Do you mind if I come over, and try a walk with him?"

"I'd love for you to do that. But I've never seen any dog wild about a leash before, he thinks it's a snake! Don't expect too much."

"I'll be there."

Of course when she arrived, Lockie loved her. Just the sweetest little puppy. Only I knew the Spirits of the Leash.

She held him, fit the harness around his chest, talking with him softly, endlessly. "There's the little Lockie! So sweet! We're going to have a walk together! Won't that be fun? You'll have your harness, your leash, and we'll walk through the forest . . ."

I hadn't talked with him as much as she did. But that talk is not where the evil spirits lay. Sabryna took a lot of little puppy-food treats with her. She picked him up, walked out of the door. "Oh, look at the sunshine! And all the trees and the birds, they'll be so happy to see you today, Lockie!"

She set him down at the forest road. Moved the leash ahead. He was stone at the end of the leash. "Here we go, on a nice walk!"

I knew he was about ready to go berserk.

But instead of tugging on the leash, she walked back to him, and she lay down on the ground next to him. "You're so brave! To have the leash on you, and the harness. Here are some treats for you!" Instead of going to the moon, he crunched on the little pieces. Came close to her. "You made a step, Lockie! Good for you! Here's some treats for you!"

Crunch, crunch . . .

She sweet-talked him, gave him treats for every blink of his eyes.

"You're such a good boy, Lockie. So good! Here are some treats for being good!"

Crunch, crunch . . .

After a while, Sabryna got up from the road, knelt near the puppy, fed him treats. And after a few minutes, she started to walk.

Oh, my, I thought. Here's the test!

She didn't tug on the leash. She took some baby steps, and would you believe, Lockie stepped with her!

"Good steps! Good walk!"

Treats.

Crunch, crunch . . .

And that was it. No snakes, no evil spirits. Lockie walked easily with her, with us. The leash never tugged him, it was loose up hills, down hills. A hundred feet, and she gave the leash to me, and there was not a squeak from Lockie. He was enjoying the walk.

We stopped when she saw some little flowers, Lockie stopped too, to admire them. Then we walked on, and the puppy trotted up the steps to the deck. More treats. Good dog,

Lockie! Good puppy!

"Call me, if you have any problems," she said.

I said, "Thank you, for what you did, Sabryna. Really. A miracle! Thank you."

She's no dog trainer.

She just loves.

*W*hat Am I Afraid Of?

*S*O MANY EVENTS, I'm finding now, ideas that I should have learned in high school.

When someone's angry, for instance, I didn't learn what one needs to say to them (except get away, to myself). Now I've learned that the question for me, if not to the Angry One, is: *What am I afraid of losing?* Anger is always fear. And fear is always about losing something that matters to us.

I am almost never angry, but when that happens and I ask what am I afraid of losing, there's an answer right top of all that emotion. I'm going to lose my freedom; I'm going to lose my right to be by myself; I'm going to lose my independence; I'm going to lose the company of a friend.

When I answer what am I afraid of, my earth mind is quick and true: "I'm going to lose my . . ." and the answer is one or two words. I can explain those words or not, I can fight (which has never physically been necessary in my life) or flee, which I've done time and again, this lifetime.

Even while I was with the Air Force, the guns were never loaded to fire at human beings . . . just targets in the wilderness. While flying, I was never angry, nor can I remember any of the other pilots angry, either. We could be frightened, but never did it jump to angry.

That was a good thing to learn, no matter how late it came for me.

Nowadays, or Thenadays, something that threatened loved-one's lives, or my own, would tick me off. Not so much now. Nothing threatens the one friend I care about, and as far as I can tell, nothing threatens my life, either.

There's an odd thing that happens to most near-death-experiencers . . . they come back from dying and they're no longer frightened of it. Maybe the definition of Death has changed for them. It has for me! It changed because there was nothing painful, waiting for me, I didn't even realize I had died. The airplane crashed and I didn't know it till a week or so later.

The illusion that I was making a wonderful soft landing on a farmer's landing strip continued for a minute after the air-plane was caught in the wires and slammed inverted onto the ground. I felt no crash, no sudden change in her flying. I was a spirit pilot in a spirit airplane, both of us perfect. I had no shadow that anything was wrong until a week later, when I woke in a hospital bed, of all places.

Nowadays, something threatens to kill me, I'm not angry: "Oh, time to go home? Fine!" My bags are packed. How is it that people hearing a medical verdict of death can keep from smiling? We're all heading home, and sorrow is a mortal's game, not a spirit's. Try it. Shift into your spirit's mind, right now, and ask if your spirit is sorrowful about dying.

What can we lose, here, as mortals? Our houses and airplanes, the things of our lives? Not necessary at home. Lose our lives? Funny . . . but impossible. Our friendships, our loves? Can't lose love from dying. It may seem to end to a mortal survivor, but it's there all at once, soon as they fly home.

A long time, being separated? Hardly. Take your memory of your life—does it seem a long time ago, when you were six or ten? It's a few minutes gone in time.

Sure enough, our belief of days going forward in time is awfully slow, like a horizon we're driving toward, in a car, while the past is lightning gone. The slow time is necessary for us to care for the details of the future.

Long waits to bear between friends? Not true at home . . . how often do dear departed friends tell us they can't wait to see us again? As far as I know, never; while we mortals can miss them terribly, year after year.

A big change for me: since the crash, the belief of death is *nothing!*

If I were going to move through an arched doorway into a room of old friends, into a delight of beliefs, into a homecoming, would it seem like a strange event for me? Welcome, certainly; but strange? Not a moment! We're there in a second, we don't miss the ones who are connected to us, the ones who stay as mortals for a while . . . we'll see them in dreams every night, which they mostly forget but we as spirit, never do.

The only times I'm afraid, now, is when I've forgotten home, and tune to the beliefs of mortals. And a mortal I guess I believe I shall be, for a while yet. Soon as I remember home, though, there's no fear.

Mortality is a lonely place for a few of us. We live since most of us promised to hang on even when we found that home is infinitely to be preferred, but leaving here is not for a single second a sad event for us. Some things to do, and do them we shall, but going home? That's a rainbow!

Questions for an Angel

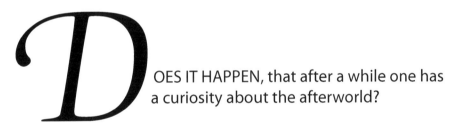

DOES IT HAPPEN, that after a while one has a curiosity about the afterworld?

Maybe some people have the curiosity, and since the blessing of my airplane crash it's been floating around, just out of touch.

"Out of touch," he said, "since you're not caring enough, right now, to know."

It was a guardian spirit. A handsome male angel. I've seen a number of guardian angels for the last year and a half. Maybe not seen, but talked with. I know they can do all sorts of things for mortals. To understate a bit: they're our friends.

"I know that I'm pretending to be a mortal just now," I said.

"Well said. 'Pretending to be.'"

It was somehow all right to ask. "I talk more easily with female spirit guides. Would you mind . . . ?"

He didn't blink. "Stand by,"

They can shift—could I shift, if I were an angel, or a guide? Well, I could get someone to change places if I weren't the right one.

"Hi. How can I help you?" What a sweet face. No wings, but so dear. As though I knew her.

"I want to know about afterlives."

"Of course," she said. "What do you need to know?"

"I was there not long ago," I said. "In one of them." After the crash.

"Afterlives. So you know, don't you? You know there's more than one heaven."

"I thought there might be more than one," I said, "because, well . . . how could everyone go to one afterworld? All those radical different beliefs?"

"Good!" She was pleased. "Our heaven is matched to our sense of Love. How long did it take you, how long to consider, that there might be more?"

I couldn't lie. "Seventy-some years," I whispered.

"You probably had lots of other things to learn."

"Airplanes," I said. "Can I ask a question?" She had long hair, a long dark pony-tail. I knew she lived in an alternate heaven.

"Of course."

"How many, do you think . . ."

She made it my question. "How many afterworlds are there, Richard, would you say? How many heavens?"

Instead of telling her, *I have no idea*, I told her my guess. "An infinite number."

"We like to say there's an indefinite number, but you'd prob- ably agree."

I smiled. "More than anyone can count." I got it right.

"And that's because . . . ?" she said.

What's a because answer? "Because everyone has a belief of what it could be for them, and they create it, same as we cre- ate our beliefs on earth." Interesting, I thought, the hereafter, it's our belief, too!

"What if they don't believe in an afterlife?" she said. "It's just blank for them? Everything's dark, forever and forever?"

"Maybe for a while it is. And then someone like you, some one they love, might mention that if they moved a little toward the light . . ."

"But it was dark."

"Because they couldn't see without a suggestion. Soon as she said, 'Toward the light,' they'd see it."

"Good." How could I be good, when the guy said I didn't do any homework? I prefer women angels.

"So there are hereafters that are hell," I said, "and some that are heaven?"

"Whatever we truly believe, that presents itself as true for us."

"So what's real? Is everything beliefs on beliefs?"

"Oh. You know that." What a smile!

"Are angels always beautiful?"

"Thank you," she said. "We are, in your heaven. The higher you rise, the beautifuller are the scenes, and the angels, too." She repeated herself. "What's real?"

"All the worlds, they're beliefs." But I knew, or at least I was convinced, "Love's real," I said.

"You don't say *God?*"

"Nope. Love."

"Time for you to wake," she said. "What a pleasure, to meet you!" She smiled, as though she had talked with me for a thousand dreams.

*Z*iggy-Zumba

I HAD JOINED the New Jersey Air National Guard in 1961, checked out as a pilot in the F-84F. A slow airplane by today's fighters, it could barely fly past Mach One. It was big and heavy, 14 tons at gross weight, it took a whole lot of runway to get the airplane up to flying speed. The Republic company called it the *Thunderstreak*, pilots called it the *Super Hog*.

I was a new pilot in the squadron, nobody knew me, nobody knew how well I could fly. Could they trust me?

Back in those days, just like today, I despised alcohol. What are pilots doing drinking that stuff, when the airplanes needed sharp minds? I never went to the McGuire Officers

Club, where they served alcohol, unless it was required. And sure enough one Friday evening it was required, a pilot's meeting at the Club for some sort of get-together and of course for drinking.

I ordered my Ginger Ale, and a couple pilots of my new squadron said, "Ginger Ale?"

I said, "Yeah."

Later in the evening, while some pilots turned drunk, I was sitting at a table talking with another about the F-84. He said the airplane had a barrier sniffer on the nose. When the sniffer sensed the end of the runway, around 130 knots, he said, the F-84F would fly. I laughed, and he did too, and I remembered, *This is not an F-86, it is not a day-fighter It is heavy, keep your airspeed up.*

About that time the rest of the squadron appeared, and stood around our table. They were humming a song. Someone took my glass of Ginger Ale and replaced it with a tall glass full to the brim of clear liquid, an olive on the bottom.

Oh, my, I thought. They'll sing their song and I'm supposed to drink all that gin in one gulp, maybe two. They began to sing.

"Hi Ziggy Zumba, Zumba, Zumba, Hi Ziggy Zumba, Zumba, Zumba Zay.

"Hold 'm down, you Zulu Warriors, Hold 'im down you Zula Chiefs,

"Hold 'm down . . ."

Time slipped cogs for me, then.

What did they want? They wanted me to forget my silly no-alcohol habit, since this is a rite for every new pilot. If he drinks, it means that he trusts us more than his strange principle and we will let him fly with us. If he doesn't drink, it means that he despises us and we'll never trust him in the air.

". . . you Zulu Warriors, Hold 'm down . . ."

I thought about that, made a decision. I will drink this glass down, and it will have no affect on me at all. My mind is not at odds with the pilots, it's with my belief that alcohol will hurt me. I will drink it down, because I'll be one of the best F-84 pilots in this squadron. I shall not be touched . . .

". . . you Zulu Chiefs. Drink! Drink! Drink!"

And I did. I lifted the glass, olive and all, and drank it down.

There was a cheer from the pilots, and a second later I knew the truth. The glass I drank was not filled with gin. It was filled with water (and an olive).

Someone there decided against filling the glass with gin, since he thought (drunk as he was) that a full glass of gin might kill a guy who didn't drink. Test 'im, learn what the song would tell us about him, and not have to drag his lifeless body into the night outside the McGuire Air Force Base Officer's Club.

It worked.

The Many-Worlds Interpretation of Heaven

IS THIS IMPOSSIBLE an event like this?

It was a dream about a dear friend, an old pilot, who had been killed in a crash years before. In the dream, I saw him with his J-3 Cub on floats, he landed on a lake and I met him when he reached the shore.

I knew that others, after they die, take the appearance of what they think was their favorite appearance while on Earth, and asked my friend why he looked just as I remember him, instead of as a young man? He said he likes being seen as the old-timer.

I flew with him in the Cub, and he pointed out toward crystal cities on the horizon ("For those who like city life," he said). Then he asked if I wanted to fly the Cub. Of course I said, Yes, please.

"Just a minute," he said. He slowed way down, then pressed the Cub into a spin, from about 2,000 ft. "OK," he said while the airplane was spinning straight down, "you've got it . . ."

I recovered, laughing.

"Do you have mid-airs here?" I asked, after a while.

"Sometimes. The airplanes just pass through each other, of course, nobody's hurt." Then in case I needed reminding, he smiled and said, "Now you don't want to do that on Earth . . ."

I asked what I could take with me from this moment, to prove this was more than my imagination or a dream. What could I tell his son to show I really talked with his dad?

He answered at once. "Ask him about Uncle Eddy." Then the scene dissolved and I woke.

I wrote later to his son:

". . . an odd thing happened that I wanted to check with you. About a month ago I had a remarkable dream about your dad. I was by a lake in the forest, not quite knowing why, when I looked up and saw a Cub on floats on downwind. It landed on the water, and it was your dad, looking just like always and really happy. I asked what he was doing here, and he said that he flew kids, mostly, to give them an intuition, before they're born, a love of flying that would later draw them into the air.

94

"We talked for a while in this dream and we flew together. It was vivid, unforgettable the whole event, and I'm still remembering it, and how glad I was to see him again.

"For some reason I wanted verification that this was a real meeting. I asked if there was anything I could say to you that would make sense, beside it was an interesting dream. He said I should ask you about Uncle Eddie. That was the end of the dream.

"I don't have a clue," I said, "what that might mean, if it means anything at all. For a while I wasn't even going to mention the dream to you. I don't know if your dad had a brother, or whether Eddie might be a dog's name, or what it meant. But finally I thought hey, I'll ask. Whether or not that name means anything to you, this remains the most memorable dream of my life."

His son's answer came the next day:

"Your dream was interesting, all right. Dad always enjoyed giving kids their first airplane ride.

"As far as 'Uncle Eddie,' the only person he may be referring to is Capt. Eddie. He was an American Airline pilot who flew for Dad at the seaplane base when he had layovers down here. Capt. Eddie owned a Piper J-3 on floats and kept it at his house.

"Odd that you mentioned it, since he just died, at the age of 93.

"Eddie flew every Saturday morning up until his death. The

last few years of his life he was very frail and kept the airplane at our seaplane base. We would help get the airplane ready for him every weekend. Capt. Eddie was still a very good pilot to the day he died.

"I never heard Dad call him anything but Capt. Eddie."

Honest, this event really happened. What do you think? How do you explain this dream? Does it need explaining?

*W*hat Happened?

"ID THAT REALLY happen? Was he a real person?"

"What you wrote, that was fiction, right?"

"Is this nonfiction or what?   It starts out I know it's real because there's a picture of you and the airplane, but then . . ."

Instead of turning Socratic, those moments: "What is Truth, my child?" I frowned.

Who was the first person with the idea to class books, to class experience, to class life itself into two categories: Fiction or Nonfiction?   Looking into the past, I see a forest of hands, "I did!"

Everybody perceives differently. One witness in court sworn to tell the truth, testifies that the defendant's auto was travelling at high speed through a red traffic light, no attempt to stop. The defendant swears of course she didn't stop because the light was green as Go! Who's lying? Nobody. Different perceptions, caught in the strobe of a half-second drama. Colors become mind-stuff.

I heard a voice in my head once long ago, while I was landing my biplane, an old machine that a pilot couldn't much see ahead. It had no radio, so the voice didn't come electrically. I was landing, concentrated on that task, enjoying it.

The voice said, "Move to the right." No emotion, just a suggestion.

Voices we hear, are they fiction? Imaginations in the mind? Not willing to debate this I moved, and one second after I stomped on the rudder and slammed my airplane to the right, another airplane shot by on the left side, landing in the opposite direction. (This story is true, by the way.)

There could have been no voice. The instant I slid to the right, the blurring flash of the other airplane, the event was done. Did the other pilot even see me? Don't know, it doesn't matter. I thought about that for years afterward.

Was that event fiction (a voice that couldn't exist) or non-fiction (a collision, for certain, set by physics, to happen).

My non-fiction belief, I thought, was that I *perceived* a voice that day, it seemed like a voice in the summer of 1970, landing at Red Oak, Iowa. Thus, acting on the fiction of a voice that could not have happened, I did not become a flaming ball of wreckage collided on the grass.

What's fiction? Some say, "The whole world's fiction! Made-up scenes, beliefs, electrical signals that we see with our brain!"

Others smile indulgently. "You can't touch 'er, she ain't real."

I like to think that meaning is "Whatever changes our thought and therefore our lives."

Fiction can change our thought—how many deer-hunters-to-be never aimed a rifle at a deer after they read *Bambi*, pure fiction; or saw the movie, nothing but a cartoon on the screen? I'm one. Never shot at a deer, or at any animal, in my life. Thanks to Felix Salten.

Fact can change our thought, too, whether or not we can define what fact is. So can dreams, data, research, beliefs, carbon analysis, illusions, ice-core samples, telepathy, errors, ghosts, hard-copy printouts, miracles, photographs, alien abductors, someone's fiction that we thought was fact, a collision on an old grass runway.

We are creatures of our perceptions. Even the walls we build to stop us from our beliefs are walls of perception, subject to Earth's perfect solvent, imagination.

So come these stories, my own history, which I believe once happened in my life. Each story moves our lives one step forward. I thought they were disconnected, scattered memories. But now, watching them all, I think that they're beautifully connected, as though they were the steps of destiny, each had to happen before the next one could exist.

Your own life may be the same way, the stories you've remembered, one after another. Are they thrown into your life by the gods, or are they footsteps that you've decided to hammer yourself, from the false recollections, from the true perceptions of memory?

$\mathcal{F}$inding Lucky

$\mathcal{L}$UCKY TOLD ME, in a dream, after he died: "If I come back to Earth, you will know it from a person who will enter our front door, and they will talk about Shetland Sheepdogs. Then you will find me, in my new body, south of your house."

I didn't believe it would happen quite this way. I thought that in all the northwest of the United States of America, south of my house, there would be a Shetland Sheepdog that would spring to life and mirror the spirit of my friend Lucky, who had died three years before.

Sure enough, for the first time in the years since his death, someone walked into the front door just as Lucky had said they would, and talked about Shetland Sheepdogs.

After being quiet for the years, not even thinking about a replacement for Lucky, all at once I remembered his dream, coming true for me and for him.

But I couldn't find him! There was not one Shetland Sheepdog I could find, nothing. I searched day after day, looking for him. Nothing. How can Shelties be so popular? Not one to be found for sale, not to mention that one would need to be a reincarnation of Lucky.

Way at the last of my wits, I scanned a puppy website that promised excellent Shelties, I saw nothing there. Lots of cute little pups, but not one that had the attitude of Lucky. How do we tell an attitude of a dog? When we've lived with them for ten years, we know their attitude: they're playful, thoughtful, courageous, they're ringing bells as a watchdog, they're a gentle king to the other creatures nearby.

Not one Shelty for sale, nearby.

But Lucky didn't mean nearby. He meant far, far to the south of the house, not in Washington State, not in the northwest, but 1,500 miles south and east of home, in the land of Missouri.

One last time, I took one final look at the puppies, and I blinked. Why didn't I see this photograph, how could I have missed it earlier? Of all the puppies, here was one, only one, who would be thinking about his new life, not paying much attention to the camera, considering it all in the way that Lucky would consider life, most of the day!

Lucky was kind to the other animals. Some of course may have stepped a little bit out of line, and might have needed a bark. A squirrel, for instance, sometimes a squirrel might have required a dash and a growl to go well up its tree. But mostly, Lucky was kind, was thoughtful.

When we got Zsa-Zsa, a very young puppy to be his partner, Lucky wondered. Do I need this little puppy in my life?

I could read his thoughts. When we go for a walk, he said to me, I'll be enjoying all nature, and Zsa-Zsa will *bite my tail!*

I tried to understand. I asked Lucky to do his best with the puppy, and he sighed. But his attitude was ironed into his spirit.

So I knew Lucky's thoughts about most any event. Zsa-Zsa had tested Lucky against bright little puppies. What if I found him now, as a puppy himself? Would he be thinking about it, would he say, I'm a puppy now, too, and I will understand this part of my life, and remember it when I'm the king of my property. I'll be kinder to young dogs. It may be necessary to bark at squirrels, but I'll be kind to puppies.

Lucky's vision of our future came true. I wonder what he will bring from the afterlife, what he will learn from this life on Earth? Will both of us discover together about our place in forever?

Such a thoughtful dog!

*I*s Television Good for Me?

*A*T FIRST, DECIDING ABOUT television was a simple matter of thoughtful grading. A slow matter, too, as I had been watching television for all these days and never thought of grading it.

How I grade: Every news event in a half-hour newscast, would earn a grade from me, its viewer. There may be fifty events or more: a newswriter's few sentences about what she feels is newsworthy, that's one event; some sentences she finds tragic is another; that she finds funny is another; a story about a person; about nature; about entertainment; about the weather; a commercial: each scrap of video is an event.

Scores:

If my spirit is lifted by what I've seen .... *Plus 1*

If my spirit is unaffected................... *Zero (0)*

If my spirit is dragged down by this .... *Minus 1*

I'll note these numbers on a piece of paper, then add them up to get a Plus (Pleasure for my spirit), a Nothing for it, or a Minus (Empty place where my spirit used to be).

At no time in my life did I respond in any way to a news event on television. It would be nice or not-nice, but never once did I write letters, mix in street demonstrations, never voted for or against, never gave or asked for money.

I planned to do this test for a few days, since I knew the results of my scores before I began. I knew that my spirit would never be lifted by news programs, by all but a few well-written and photographed programs. If my grades were deep in Minus Territory, why was I wasting my spirit on television? Wouldn't Quiet be a better background for my life, than some vast Minus television score?

Better I use a video screen to see videos, knowing I have to choose them first, and they'll matter to me, and most likely be positive.

Then before I began my grading began, something happened that confirmed my grades. The World Trade Towers collapsed.

It took me a few seconds to realize that the world in the United States would be changed. I knew that if I kept the television set, that I would see the first scenes of the collapse thousands and thousands of times. That the news would be full of it, there would be rings of death and war rippling out from Ground Zero.

Years of controversy, years of lies, efforts to find truth, efforts to crush new evidence of the event. I didn't think of the number of young mortals of our military who would die, and the number of whatever we decided would be the population of Theirs to die. I didn't think of the money that would be earned for the companies who manufactured the tools of war. I didn't think what a great way to earn billions of dollars for war denominated companies! I could have thought about that, but I didn't.

Instead, I put the television set into the back of the pickup truck and left it at the recycling center.

Here is my television set today:

In these years, have I been sorry I missed the newscasts? No. The missed the entertainments? No. The situation dramas and comedies? No.

Would I have liked some of the programs I never saw? Probably. I didn't feel sad for not seeing them, I just didn't know they were on the invisible channels for my non-existent television screen.

Only recently have I received broadcasts, usually about food and exercise from a transmitter you've seen before:

Aside from this, gradually, the Internet gave a small part of the world that I half-way cared about. I heard about the tsunami, about the Japanese nuclear meltdown, about the Malaysian airliner on the web. Did I do anything about these events? No.

My world became local. The little towns nearby continued through all the crises with not even a tremble from the world's earthquakes. I got to know the forest nearby, noticed when the sun rose and set, when the moon turned about the earth. I wrote about a world much more important to me than the television reports.

I lifted my days on some events that changed me, but they were never on the channels. I flew off-airways in small aircraft. I had a crash that taught me that no matter what happens in space-time, nobody dies. Horrors and tragedies in daily life here on Earth, they don't much matter to our friends in the afterlife, those worlds where we live for countless multi millions of what we would call years. As mortals, we can decide whether any event is a tragedy or a delight or both: a belief of ours.

I've changed my consciousness from television to the Internet and to books and personal life.

I've discovered that Lockie, my Shetland Sheepdog, is capable of finding a small half of a candy bar that was hidden behind a computer on a table that would not support his weight without collapsing . . . it was not possible for him to have retrieved that candy bar. But he did. I was not aware he had left the kitchen when he disappeared to make that remarkable retrieval.

Is that story ever going to be on television? I hope not. Has my spirit been lifted from the books I've read? Balloon-like has it lifted. Lots of books on death and dying, lots of computer information about crop circles, aliens, events that may even touch you when I put them on the website, offered for your interest, from mine.

How do I think about politics? I don't think about politics. At all. If at some day politics touches my world, decides that I am a loss to their world, that's fine. Destroy writers, political leaders may say, extinguish my belief in life as a mortal? Certainly, if they wish. Destroying our bodies or not, by one or by millions, there's no person or event who has the power to kill me or you or any expression of life (I learned that from my airplane crash).

There are thousands of, part of me says millions of, television news stories I've never seen. I don't know about murders, about all sorts of crime, about terrible accidents, about natural events that kill and displace humans. Senseless political events that kill so many others, I've never heard of them. Does it hurt me, that I haven't been told about them, and so many others that never made it into the news? No. If I had a chance to go back through the last ten years and learn about them, would I do it? Nope.

This world, just like others, like planets, like heavens everywhere, is a belief for those of us who accept them. We play with our beliefs, shift them, change them, dance with space-times till they cannot teach us more, and then we fly into dimensions where we can learn other things that we've never heard about.

All these beliefs of mine, I didn't have them in my daily consciousness when I started this lifetime. Gradually gradually, year after year, a web of light spun around me as they do for most everyone. Ideas that made sense to me, they stayed. They fit like puzzle pieces into the other pieces which had stayed, too. Right now I'm learning a difficult lesson—that loneliness is a self-imposed belief. That we have others who we've cared for and who care for us, though perhaps not one of them has a body in space-time.

Can't some of them be still wearing a body? Of course they can. I think I've been learning that when we stop trying to meet one other who will change our life, it will happen by itself.

Do I know that's true, body or not? Yes. And that it will be a surprise? Without question.

Do I enjoy it? Not a bit. Yet again, slowly slowly, I'm learning how to touch a loved one with no body at all. How to let a spirit visit my mind. Gradually I'm learning a lesson we've had time and again – how to live in a spiritual world even while we believe in space and time for our lessons. Every lifetime we decide, regardless of others, regardless even in this age of television, who controls the adventures of our lives.

How much patience, how much care we pour, into our education!

*T*oday is the Day!

TODAY IS THE PUB DATE of the New Edition of *Jonathan Livingston Seagull*. It's the complete edition, now, since it includes a Part 4, that I had written immediately after Part 3, years ago, but never published with the first parts. It didn't get published since I thought it was just not proper at the time, it was something in the future of the flock (and in the world of humans), that would never happen.

I thought I had thrown Part 4 away, and I did. But a few months ago, Sabryna was going through old files and she found a typewritten carbon copy of Part 4. She visited me, asked if I knew what she had found.

I said no. Then I couldn't stand her silence, "What did you find?"

And there in her hand was the old writing, and I remembered it. Times had changed, and now Part 4 was germane to the story, and the publisher agreed. So now it's on sale.

I remembered what had happened when the story was published. I flew around the country, talking about the book for those who cared, signing copies. Looking back now, I'm sure that I must have autographed at least . . . a dozen copies of the book for readers. Could have been more.

And now, for one of the first times, I sent autographed copies to readers and two of them never found their owners! One was international, but I've sent international copies for all these years and they managed to get where they wanted to go.

Yesterweek, the publisher had sent me 20 copies of the new edition, and they were lost! I've now stopped signing books, for all the expense of money and time sending books and they never arrive, it's not worth the owner's time, or even mine.

I remembered, though, what I thought about autographed copies. I remembered the first time I saw Antoine de Saint-Exupery's signature on a thousand-dollar copy of *The Little Prince*. One can learn much about a person from their signature, and I saw his small careful signature, almost hand-printed letters, on the page—a person who cared about details!

I never would have guessed that Saint-Exupery cared about

details, I thought he might have been a pilot who subscribes to the old-time caution: "Kick-the-tires, Light-the-fires and First-one-off-is-the-Leader." Not only do I know some pilots like that, I'm sort of like that, myself. But not Saint-Ex. So though I couldn't afford to buy that signature (now one's for sale at $140,000), I never forgot it.

Today, I thought that there may have been someone like me who puzzles over autographs. What was I going to do, now that I've stopped sending books? It took me a while, but you knew the answer before I did. Could I print an autograph on the website?

My signature has been printed in several books, so it was there anyway, it wasn't any secret, but the art that I shared with most autographs, that was not printed. Why not an autograph (which with a few hours of studying handwriting practice, will tell you everything about me) on the web?

Saint-Ex and I loved flying, all right, but our signatures are as far apart as two asteroids. His is careful, thoughtful, yearning to describe who that magnificent pilot could be. Mine is . . . different.

So you have here two autographs.

And,

One is for fliers and the other is for . . . fliers, too. Of course you will understand what every line means. Why are there always seven rays from the sun, I wonder?

*A*n Odd Feeling

H AS THIS EVER HAPPENED to you? For years my Shelties have been sweet little dogs. They'll bark, of course, since they're so good at watch-dogging, and you love them for that.

Yet little Lockie, grown now from a puppy to a powerful dog, sometimes in the night, I'll be typing on my computer in bed, like now, and something strange happens.

Instead of concentrating on my next sentence, I will have this uncanny feeling: I need to give some treats to my dog.

A few minutes of this and I can't write at all. I must get up, go into the kitchen and give treats to Lockie! It's midnight, I glance at my companion and he's just watching me . . .

Has this ever happened to you?

$\mathcal{R}$oofs and Stars

$\mathcal{D}$O YOU KNOW how hard it is to live in a house?

Difficult, very difficult. If you want to see the stars, your problem is the roof. The roof will cover just about any star in the night sky. A roof is very nice if it's raining, or snowing, but when you want to see the stars, a roof is a bother.

I went onto the Internet, of course, and began planning. If I'm in my bed at night (and there's Lockie, too—though he doesn't spend much time looking at stars when there are pillows to be shredded), what are my options?

(My ceiling, pre-screen)

Have the roof move, is one choice. The roof of the observatory on Mount Palomar moves for just that reason. Yet, in the house I live in, not only the roof but most of the walls would have to roll away to get, say, 160 degrees of stars over my bed.

I thought about it for half an hour or so, and then decided that retracting the roof would be just too expensive.

My Plan B is a camera on top of the house. It would need to be in a clear glass dome, and the camera would be an all-sky unit. That could be way easier than retracting things. The few cables from the camera would come to a video screen on the ceiling of my bedroom. A problem began there. What size of the screen would I need?

(Potential screen for the ceiling.)

It would have to be the whole ceiling, I thought, or at least, say 12 feet by 12 feet over the bed. That would take, say 16 three-foot screens bolted into to the drywall.

Securely bolted.

There is a scene in *Heaven can Wait*, that shows what happens when a huge mirror falls from the ceiling to the bed. Fortunately, Warren Beatty had just tossed a briefcase on the bed when the mirror crashed, so he wasn't killed.

Then.

Securely bolted.

The Planar PS5560 Ultra Slim LCD Display video screen is 55 inches by 30 inches wide, a little bigger than the units I had considered. It costs $4,152.99 for each one, $66,447.84 for all screens, then the camera, wiring and the securing, about $89,000 for the entire system.

I hoped it would show stars down to the sixth magnitude, like an human eye, but third magnitude was about the best the camera could send in a dark night. There was nothing, at any price that could put the sky I wanted to see on my ceiling.

Then Sabryna came to lunch one day, and I told her about my plan. Did she think that two cameras, linked together somehow, could they bring it up to sixth magnitude stars? Or would a light intensifier tube be fitted to the wiring after the camera and before the video screens, would that work? Would they be fast enough to show a UFO moving through or would UFOs be just a dim blur on my screen?

She thought about my plan, and then said, "Couldn't you just take a blanket and sleep on the deck?"

(Sabryna's Plan.)

I thought about that:

I'd have 170 degrees sky coverage north-south and 160 degrees east-west.

I'd have sixth magnitude stars.

I'd have full-vision display of all UFOs, anywhere in the sky.

There would be no possibility of video screens crashing on me.

There were no cameras in her plan, no video at all, no wiring.

It would save $89,000.

Lockie could sleep there, too, plus he could bark at the UFOs, an Extra-Terrestrial Warning Unit that my plan had never considered.

(The ETWU, in daylight.)

"If it rains, though," I said.

"Would the cameras work," she said, "if it were raining?"

No, I thought, they wouldn't work.

A blanket. Sometimes two minds can figure things out better than just one.

Teaching the Person We Used to Be

I'M NOW READING a book (Biocentrism) which suggests that life creates the universe, not the other way round.

I wrote a book like that years ago, in three pages. It's in the story of my friendship with the me when I was ten years old. It's about my discovery of why things work in space and time. The reasons for the book don't matter here, but the conversation does.

Here's a page when I walked with young Dickie into a grocery store, and told him about how our belief works in spacetime. I had to invent a few words.

****

"Sometimes I wish you were a grownup, Dickie."

"Why?"

Interesting, I thought, picking a handful of beets. Not a murmur of distress when I wished for a change impossible for him to make. "Because I could explain in a lot fewer words if you knew quantum mechanics. I've whittled the physics of consciousness down to a hundred words, but you're going to have to puzzle over it forever. You're never going to be a grown-up, and I'll never be able to hand you my tract that fits on one page."

Curiosity prevailed. "Pretend I'm a grown-up who loves quantum mechanics," he said. "How would you say how consciousness works in one page? I'm too little to understand, of course, but it would be fun to hear. Say it as complicated as you want."

He's daring me, I thought, he thinks I'm bluffing. I turned the shopping cart toward the checkout stand.

"First I'd say the title: The Physics of Consciousness—or—Spacetime Explained."

"Next you'll tell me the abstract," he said.

I looked at him. I didn't know about abstracts until after I had run away from school. How could he know?

"Right," I said. "And now I have to talk in fine print, the way they do in *The American Journal of Particle Science*. Listen tight, and maybe you'll understand a word or two, child though you may be."

He laughed. "Child though I may be."

I cleared my throat, slowed the cart and stopped near the cash register, glad for the minute's wait in line. "You want to hear this right straight through, all at once?"

"As if I was a quantum mechanic," he said.

Instead of correcting his grammar, I told him what I thought. "We are focus-points of consciousness," I said, "enormously creative. When we enter the self-constructed hologrammetric arena we call space-time, we begin at once to generate creativity particles, *imajons*, in violent continuous pyrotechnic deluge. Imajons have no charge of their own, but are strongly polarized through our attitudes and by the force of our choice and our desire into clouds of *conceptons*, a family of very-high-energy particles which may be positive, negative, or neutral."

He listened, pretended he could understand.

"Some positive conceptons are *exhilarons, excytons, jovions*. Common negative conceptons include *gloomons, tormentons, tribulons, agonons, miserons*.

"Indefinite numbers of conceptons are created in nonstop eruption, a thundering cascade of creativity pouring from every center of personal consciousness. They mushroom into *concepton clouds*, which can be neutral or strongly charged—buoyant, weightless or leaden, depending on the nature of their dominant particles.

"Every nanosecond an indefinite number of concepton clouds build to critical mass, then transform in quantum bursts to high-energy probability waves radiating at tachyon speeds through an eternal reservoir of supersaturated alternate events. Depending on their charge and nature, the probability waves crystallize certain of these potential events to match the mental polarity of their creating consciousness into holograph appearance. Are you following me, Dickie?"

He nodded, and I laughed.

"The materialized events become that mind's experience, freighted with all the aspects of physical structure necessary to make them real and learningful to the creating consciousness. This autonomic process is the fountain from which springs every object and event in the theater of spacetime.

"The persuasion of the imajon hypothesis lies in its capacity for personal verification. The hypothesis predicts that as we focus our conscious intention on the positive and life-affirming, as we fasten our thought on these values, we polarize masses of positive conceptons, realize beneficial probability waves, bring useful alternate events to us that otherwise would not have appeared to exist.

"The reverse is true in the production of negative events, as is the mediocre in-between. Through default or intention, unaware or by design, we not only choose but create the visible outer conditions that are most resonant to our inner state of being.

130

"The end."

He waited while I paid for the groceries. "That's it?" he said.

"Is it wrong? Have I erred in any way?"

He smiled, for Dad had taught us both how important it is to pronounce that word correctly. "How can I tell if you erred, child that I am?"

"Laugh if you must," I told him, "go ahead and call me a zany. But in a hundred years somebody's going to print those words in *Modern Quantum Theory* and nobody's going to think it's mad."

He stepped on the frame of the shopping cart, rode along as I pushed it to the car. "If you don't get trapped by gloomons," he said, "that will probably happen."

****

Today is not a hundred years but only twenty from the day I wrote those pages. Here now are at least two books: *The Physics of Consciousness*, by Evan Harris Walker, and *Biocentrism*, by Robert Lanza. They may suggest something similar to the chapter in *Running from Safety*.

Does the smallest wish I have to go home, twenty years after writing my own little *Physics of Consciousness*, is my wish directed by gloomons? Or can jovions touch us in the same way?

A Special Meeting of Spirit Guides

A NEW EXPERIENCE, for me.

For the last several years, wishing for a dear female friend, I found that wishing is not sanctioned by a culture which measures age. It used to be, that I'd wish for someone to touch my life and sure enough, I'd find someone perfect. Now I find that if we've lost our dear friend after many years, we're supposed not to care, any more, for anyone. In these times, lacking a friend, I gradually became ready to die. At least this decision brought a meeting of my spirit guides.

"Isn't it about time for me to die?" I said, a thought in my mind after a long talk now forgotten.

"So long as you have a gift to give," one of the spirits said, "it isn't time for dying."

How many times, I thought, have friends in spirit said that to mortals? "Is that true?" I said. "There have been millions who had gifts to give, and they got to die."

At the left of the long curved table in front of me, a young spirit spoke. Not words, of course, just thoughts. "You know nothing about the understanding of the millions, but you're telling us there was no reason for them to die?"

Oh, I thought. Did I speak too soon? "Maybe not for millions, I don't know. But I knew my brother."

A gentle response from a wise one. "Did you know his agreement? Did you talk with him about it? Did you suggest that he could change his plans?"

"I was his little brother!" I said. "I didn't know anything about contracts!"

The silence was their answer. I retreated. "Well, he could have told me, at least."

Soft words, from a lovely spirit, "If you were Bobby, would you have told little ten-year-old Dickie that it was time for you to die?"

My turn for silence. Long silence. Then a whisper I could barely hear, ". . . no."

"Do you think he might have known you were going to be all

right? The less you knew, the better you'd feel? His belief of dying, and yours, do you know it's all part of your plan?"

I thought about that. Did my brother have a plan? Do I? His plan he remembered, and mine, I've forgotten?

A gentle reminder. "Mortals are sometimes impatient. You have a few little tests yet to finish. You've done most of them all these years, as you say. It's no failure if you choose to die now."

"Remember what I said, in a book? That most of us die by accident or illness? Suicide was the way for Jesus, but not for me. I haven't made that many enemies, I hope, and it's not important for them to kill me. The only thoughtful way I can think of dying, these days, is by ascending. In perfect health, a decision to let this world go, and I leave my belief of a body to vanish in the air."

A careful response. "You can do that. Have you practiced, to make it happen?"

"No."

"Have you studied, do you know from a book, or from a friend in spirit, what you need to make an ascension happen?"

"No."

A different voice. "Do you know that every death is an ascension? A trail of decisions and all at once . . ."

"So accidents," I said, "illness, those are ascensions, too?"

"They are decisions to leave one world for another."

"I don't agree. They're failures, to me. I'll fail too, if I'm tired enough, lonely enough. I would prefer ascending, if you don't mind. If you do mind, a conventional death will be fine for me. Not perfect, but good enough."

A voice from the right of the table. "Have you thought about what would happen in the minds of other mortals if you ascended?"

"No, I haven't. Do I care?"

Silence.

"Do you want me to think about that now?"

"Just quickly, that would be good for us to hear."

"Quickly. If people saw me ascending, or if I ascended alone?"

"If you ascend alone, it will be called illness. Heart failure, stroke, accident . . ."

"So I'll have some visitors," I said. "Then I'll just leave my body . . . Well, I'd have to sit down, or they'll say the fall killed me. So I'll be nice and comfortable in a chair, and my spirit leaves: a burst of light, and my body gets all sparkly, and it's gone."

"That's it?"

"I think that's it, yes."

"Your friends will tell the story about that? 'And then in a bright light, Richard just left his body! There were sparkly things and his body vanished."

Uh-oh. I sensed trouble coming.

"Your friends, they'd tell the truth?"

"Yes. Of course they will," I said. "Something like that."

Silence.

"Is that OK?" I said. "The truth . . ."

"Has anyone done that? In a hundred years? A thousand? Ever? Do you know anyone who ever ascended at the end of their life? What you call the end of your life."

"Some say it's happened . . ."

"Pretend, now. If *you* did this thing, would you be considered a normal human being? 'And his body turned all sparkly.' Is that normal, for mortals?"

"I'll ask them not to tell about that."

"It's that or the heart failure, a stroke. You said they have to tell the truth."

"Truth. OK."

The lovely one again. "And when they saw your ascension, you would not be . . . human, would you? You'd be an advanced spirit-person, or an alien. Not a human being like everyone else."

"Well if I ascended, it's a reasonable way to leave. I hate just dying like . . ."

She finished my sentence. ". . . like human beings."

"OK," I said. "So what?"

Silence.

If everyone who heard the news of my ascending, I thought, they'd think I'd been a spiritual Somebody. Not a human.

Silence. Then, "Go on. Finish your thought experiment."

So I'm not a human being, I thought. I'm one who seemed like a human for years, but wasn't. I was not one of us. My life would be seen as a mystery . . . after all, he didn't die, like mortals do, he *ascended!* He had this non-human sort of sparkly body, and a supernatural mind. Every word he wrote, they were not for us to read, there's no point in playing with the ideas. None of what he lived can possibly apply to plain-vanilla human beings. All his life, all those ideas he wrote, but *they don't apply to us!*

"Oh," I said. "So I sense that you'd prefer for me to forget the ascension."

Silence.

"In that case, I guess I'd prefer to skip it."

Silence.

"I care about what I've written, more than I care about ascending. That doesn't seem quite fair, but . . ."

"It's your choice."

"Maybe I couldn't do it, ascending."

"Maybe you couldn't," the one at the left said.

"But if I did . . ."

"No one would believe you were human."

"Oh. Is this your test for me," I said. "This your Test Number 2405?"

"You thought of this one," a spirit said, "the ascension. We don't number your tests."

'Cause there's so many of yours, I thought. The meeting was nearly over.

"Anything else?" a guardian asked. "Anything you're having trouble with, for now?"

"Well, about the woman . . ."

There was a sigh from one of the guides. "Do you want us to ask her to knock on your door? You just decided not to ascend, your own choice of what nobody's done. But you can't somehow find a way to meet your amazing woman, with all the technology . . . If you really wanted to meet each other, somehow we think you and she . . . we think you could do that on your own."

In the silence, the guides nodded, one after another. They agreed. We could do that.

I didn't agree. If I wanted to be un-lonely, though, if that was my top priority . . . well, maybe.

My spirit guides vanished, and I woke and found human furniture, around me in the room, not the curved table. I was back in my belief of earth, once again. I sighed. Had I agreed for a conventional death, for the sake of the books? Sure enough, I had.

This one, my belief of the woman, was she not my destiny, was she a personal whim of mine? And am I her whim, too, or was our meeting designed to be a test? The spirits said no. What if she's a spirit already? How can I find her, then?

Like so many other mortals, I need to think about that.

*U*nder the Stars

*L*AST NIGHT I STAYED at a little bedroom with a big skylight three feet over the bed, lots of windows and stars. That took me back to the days I used to sleep in the back yard with my telescope and watch the sky.

It was then when I saw (I think) a pair of UFOs. It was at midnight, clear and dark, no moon. It was the Fall of 1951, no satellites, then. I was nodding at my constellations when, south of Lyra, moving from west to east, came two star-colored lights, in formation, about as bright as second magnitude stars, and way up high. No sound, no contrails, and faster than any airplane then or now. They flew some 130 – 140 degrees, from one edge of the sky to the other, in three, maybe four seconds. Then gone.

I haven't seen any UFOs since that night.

Years later I flew with the Air Force for a while, went through gunnery school southeast of Phoenix, less than an hour by F-86F from Las Vegas. Learned some things I'd remember forever, but wouldn't even think about till I opened a book two days ago.

Millennial Hospitality Is one of five books by Charles Hall. They are detailed stories of his life in 1967- 1968, when he was an Air Force weather observer in the desert north of Las Vegas. He had quite a few encounters with what he called the Tall White aliens, not far from the gunnery ranges used by the pilots of Nellis AFB.

I'm reading the second of his books now. Fascinating (to me), in spite of the unending details of his stories. Fascinating? Why?

Because he wrote about details that I remembered from the gunnery range. I believed that he had in fact lived some of his story, that he had personally been there. He wrote about skip-bombing on the ranges, for instance, something as far as I know no one else finds important enough to mention. He wrote about picking up bombs to recycle them (who would write about the bombs, except those who knew they were 25-pound solid iron practice bombs, with a shot-gun smoke shell in the nose to mark where they struck the ground). He wrote about the air-to-air targets that were dropped after each session with aerial gunnery pilots. Nobody writes about these things . . . they were tucked under fifty years of flying for me and they were part of his life at the time. It would have taken days, working on a gunnery range, even to know the details.

He said he was there for two years, and the aliens he wrote about might have been real. It was the first account about the aliens, apart from the stories that they're abducting and releasing us from time to time. Those stories are probably true, but they don't tell us much about who the aliens may be. Nothing about what frightens them, how they protect themselves, who they think we are, what kind of humor they like, what happens when they go to Las Vegas, what they buy, whom they love, their anti-gravity units, what's in it for them by coming to Earth, what humans they talk with, why they're kind to us, why they kill us, sometimes.

North of Las Vegas/Henderson, of course, are the supposedly secret Areas 51, 53, 54 . . . and there are some 850 reports of sightings listed by the National UFO Reporting Center.

See http://www.nuforc.org/webreports/ndxlNV.html . We can see reports in any American states by changing the NV (Nevada) in the address to the abbreviation of any state. Click on the date to see the full report. How many people, do you think, see some UFO and then call a number to report it? I never thought to do that, so there could be a lot more events than listed there.

Reading Mr. Hall's recollection takes some patience, but he will tell you his ideas about the Tall White (Nordic) aliens. He said that he was the only person allowed to wander about the aliens resort in the desert. "Wander about" is done with some care. If you see one, he says, don't you dare try to approach them or touch them (or even worse don't try to touch their children) without specific permission from them to walk closer. I sense that this much of his books is true. I'm willing to be wrong on that, but I enjoy having a little information now, and I'll update it whenever I can.

It's easy for me to discount the author's accounts of his successful experiences, guiding two 707's and later, a flight of F-105s by relayed instructions to land in terrible weather. Those could be true. Yet somehow I don't doubt his accounts of the aliens and their human comrades at the high echelons of the Air Force. It's top secret, apparently, for the military, but the aliens don't care what we know. They allowed him (I guess by not killing him) to talk about all his experiences to anyone. Once you make an agreement with a Tall White alien, he said, you must never break your word! The Air Force had no choice but to agree with the aliens that Mr. Hall could say whatever he liked for as long as he lived. Not one comment from the military to silence a former weather observer about his top secret life, as he writes, as he talks about aliens (see "youtube charles hall"). Hoping, perhaps, that no one would believe him. I don't think he's making it up.

I'm learning much from his books, as gradually decades of official denial erodes by so many books of personal experience, by my days in the Air Force, and by his.

I doubt that I shall ever see a Tall White alien. Of course I may never see a Kodiak bear cub in the wilds of Alaska, but I'm reminded by friends from there not to hug the cute little bears when their mom is in sight. Treat grizzly bear cubs with the same distant courtesy as we've learned to greet aliens from other planets, Mr. Hall writes. I think that's good advice.

And I wonder about the aliens.

144

A New Family

I AM SO SLOW!

All my life there have been bright and clear events, all of them happening in plain sight, but I haven't noticed them, till all of a sudden now. They've never been secrets, they're like friendly dogs, going for walks with me year after year, and I never noticed.

How many events are there? Hundreds, thousands? You've been aware of most of our event companions, unless like me you're part of that two percent who never got the word.

Want an example? Here's one I noticed yesterday. Just noticed it! Yet it's been walking with me since I was maybe eight years old.

Yesterday, I noticed that we have a public family, one that we grow with. For years, the people of this family were older than we are, since we find them when we're pretty young, ourselves. We meet them in movies: Cary Grant, Katherine Hepburn, Humphrey Bogart, Elizabeth Taylor, James Stewart, Audrey Hepburn, Gary Cooper, Ingrid Bergman, Paul Newman, Rita Hayworth, Gregory Peck.

In books my family was L. Frank Baum, Margaret Mitchell, Ray Bradbury, Laura Ingalls Wilder, E.B. White, Ayn Rand, Ernest Hemingway, Antoine de Saint-Exupery, Harper Lee, John Steinbeck.

In time we'll meet others as old as we are, then a few who are younger. Our public family is these and more: singers, dancers, comedians, commentators, a few politicians, the ones who play in the theater of media. They make us smile, mostly, their wit and their skill at their craft, their sudden rise in our consciousness, and sometimes their fall. Quite a gift, this family, and we're not even aware it's a gift till they're gone.

Slowly, in time, our public family dies. Do you remember Nevil Shute? A magnificent author for me, and a best-selling writer in the 1950's. He wrote *On the Beach*, a book that may have pushed the world away from a nuclear war. Only old readers remember him, now.

Live long enough, and we'll notice that our family has disappeared, and some of us have chosen not to be part of the major modern family, a culture sometimes of hopeless drugs and wars and lies.

New actors, of course, new music groups appear where the old family was, and for some of us, remembering what lived before, they're not our family at all. The actors don't touch us as once actors did; what they call rap is not music for us, their literature gone coarse. Sometimes we don't smile at the public family as once we did.

Is the Internet a new family? I remember, for instance, it was yesterday when we believed that we fought a world war to save civilization. Does the Web tell us now what television does not mention, that the USA is involved today, for instance, in 74 wars? On the Internet, we can find out.

Like the survivors of Ray Bradbury's *Fahrenheit 451*, a few of us refuse to cheer Presidents as they murder others at weddings and funerals around the world.

Has it made me an orphan, my decision to leave a dysfunctional public family? Who is there today, to become our family? Just a few? Just Us?

Maybe that's how it works.

Reality Part Two — A Final Exam for Mortals

OW DO WE KNOW what's real?

I was walking with Lockie yesterday and for a minute I did what I did as a boy, I had a double image of him. So long as I could cross my eyes, I saw two Lockies side by side running through the meadow. Yet there was only one of them in my life, so I wondered: which image was the real one?

The two alert Shetland Sheepdogs in my vision looked exactly the same, their fur and colors and tipped ears just the same, the gold meadow was the same, the trees in each image were the same. Each of them would occasionally come to me if I called, each would eat a little treat for them if they came, with exactly the same number of crunches and with the same hope for another treat when they finished the first.

While they ignored my call, since there was a bunny that needed to be chased, I quit trying, uncrossed my eyes and watched their two images change to one. The question remained: The double image I saw, which one was the real Lockie? I reached deep into the past to find out.

I was an amateur astronomer when I was fifteen years old. I built a six-inch F9 Newtonian reflecting telescope on an equatorial mount, set on the ground in my back yard. Amazing, I thought, watching the moon, Saturn, Jupiter, Mars. On a very quiet night, after the air cooled and I could use a high-power eyepiece, I could see Syrtis Major on Mars and for a few seconds I could see a few of the *canali* there. In English the word meant *channels* but in that time, it was bent to mean *canals on Mars!*

Later that year I worked with my friend O. Richard Norton, later to become a professional astronomer. Two kids, we were, making telescope mirrors in the shop of Thomas Cave, an expert on Mars. He would make drawing after drawing (a time exposure on an earthbound telescope would blur the details of an image), showing the polar caps, the continents and the canals. Hundreds of drawings, mirrored in the drawings of serious astronomers across the country.

Years later came the cameras of spacecraft to Mars. No *canali,* anywhere! Were they a mass illusion, spread across us all for years? Tom Cave said in print later on: "We in America for the 85 years since the so-called 'canals' were discovered had seen at best illusions." All his years of work, all those drawings, illusions? Were my two Lockies illusions, too? Were they both real? Or like *canali*, were none of them?

The events that we share here, they're real, they're events in our lives. The woman who wrote that her automobile instantly jumped *backward* from the path of an oncoming semi truck. Kate's sister appeared to her, talked with her, while her family was there, no one noticed her but Kate. The accounts of other loved ones seen after they died. Photos on YouTube of orbs that made crop circles in a few seconds. UFO's seen by some in a crowd, but not seen by everyone. Which is real, the lives of those who lived these events, or the beliefs of the ones who didn't?

We can puzzle over a chess problem, then all of a sudden there's a brilliant flash of mind, a handkerchief whipped away to reveal the solution by an inner magician . . . there's the answer! Was the problem real or not?

When Elias Howe dreamed his sewing machine needle, dreamed the hole in the *point* of the needle, was it his sleeping imagination, unreal, that shifted into reality?

When we remember fragments of an old movie, is our memory real or not? If we don't remember quite right, is the scene that touched us unreal?

The events of the afterlife aren't miraculous. Many accounts suggest that we can live anywhere we wish, we create ideas for our environments, we don't need to eat or to sleep (unless we want to), we have spirits that can travel faster than light. These are natural in their own world, no one mentions them as odd—but is that reality, when we've come home to the afterworld again?

When I saw the rainbow aura of a forest burning with light, one time, never again, was it real or imagination? When Moses saw his "burning bush," when religious figures in literature, when a thousand others see sudden visions, are the visions real?

If two people, meeting minds, fall in love, and spend a day or a lifetime together, is their feeling for each other, is it real?

Do we need to concern ourselves about reality? When our unique experiences suggest that we live in a different world from anyone else, and they live in a different world from ours, is that true? Do we care whether we live in our own world with such fascinating events? Would it be possible for us to live in a stranger's world?

Does our personal sense of life care one bit for what happens in space and time?   Does it care for what others feel, what seems real to them?

Events which change our life, illusions they be, or real, do they matter? If someone is certain that evil spirits affect our lives, or that storms come from the sky-gods, does that change our world? When a cosmologist declares that the Big Bang is the one final truth of our universe, do we believe that?

Do we decide, from a lifetime of living on this planet, what is true for us and what isn't?

All our physical senses, do *they* inform us about reality? Our startling imaginations playing in our minds, do they inform us about reality? If not, what is it, that they sense?

Have you answered these questions correctly? Good.

Who are you?

$\mathcal{T}$wo Years Since

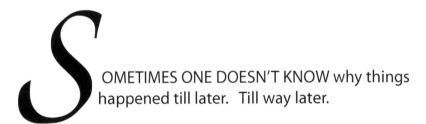

SOMETIMES ONE DOESN'T KNOW why things happened till later. Till way later.

So it was two years ago that I crashed Puff into some high-tension wires. I guess you know the story, in one second her wheels were caught in the cables and she slammed upside down into the ground, and I got to rest for most of a year, rebuilt Puff like new again and have been flying since. It's old history, yet I think of it, from time to time. I've learned some lessons for me, but was there a story for anyone else, did my little adventure help anyone else's lifetime?

All at once, the answer. Only three words, built from personal experience. Startling they are, but I think they're true, they're non-fiction:

We don't die!

Most people who have lived through the adventure speak one time or two, for their family, their own story: "I knew I was going to die, but I didn't. I don't mean in this accident, this lifetime. I mean we don't die, ever."

Thoughts and spirits change in such calm words . . . spoken, sometimes whispered in quiet times, at home. Listening, we try to share that feeling, and once in a while, we do.

What happens for the person who lived it is that we've just whispered the most important story we can tell, it means so much to us when someone understands what happened.

It doesn't matter whether someone tells me or not—well, it does matter to me—but their telling says that something happened, that a wall came down that had been years standing.

So here's a message from Adina, she lives in Sweden:

"I was reading a translated interview with you in the Swedish Magazine Inspire, and wanted to tell you that what you shared there means a lot to me.

"34 years ago my father died in an airplane crash together with 3 others. Similarly to what you were describing, the plane got caught and went straight down. They had flown from England to Sweden and were just about a kilometer from the airport, but had somehow gotten lost and were running out of fuel.

"I've thought about how they were experiencing their final hour and wondered if they even understood what happened going into the crash. What you shared in the article I've never heard of before, and it's comforting to think that even though there must have been a lot of stress before the actual crash, the crash itself can have been a completely different experience."

If I could talk with Adina, I'd say, "Yes! It was a completely different experience! Not what the newspapers said, not what anybody said! Completely different! Astonishing! Beautiful!"

Used to be, I believed in continuing lives, they made sense, they seemed rational. I don't believe, now. I know. Every death ends in a dream.

I think that the afterlife seems realer than this lifetime, yet I'm pretty sure that our afterlife is a dream, too. I *think* it is. I don't remember living it, but it makes sense, it seems rational. My guess? We live in beliefs of spacetime until we finally discover they're good lessons, but they're not real. That happens, I think, when we know that the only thing that's real, is Love.

Maybe that's wrong. If that's wrong, I have such an incredible number of lives before I can think of something higher than that.

The Three Languages

I WAS THINKING THIS morning, writing with a friend, and realized all of a sudden that beyond our normal verbal language there are three other languages we can understand. We hear messages from the body, messages from the spirit, and last from the soul. The last two use our own thoughts for its language.

The body speaks of fear and danger and death, the monkey chatter of words in all the languages of mortal minds. Other physical things, too, like challenge, like striving, like sex, it's a joy and sometimes a distress when it speaks.

Spirit speaks the subtle and unexpected, the voice beyond words. Our friends on the Other Side, guardian angels, our highest right, speak spirit, sudden inspiration, a warning from time to time, as comments from them come to keep our body and our highest aspirations going.

Soul speaks life and love, untouched by beliefs, uncaring about the fate of our body. When we think we're dying, it loves us, speaks to us then and ever. Love, I think, is the highest language there is.

On the Other Side, in the Beyond, there's no carrier language since there's no body, no physical senses are required. Thought only, telepathy, not a word of human language at all, so we can talk with our beliefs of animals, trees, flowers, all the same connection to everyone. When our Beyond self speaks from time to time with a mortal, it speaks thoughts, and we translate thoughts into our own human language . . . perfectly normal for us.

Can this be true for you? It was startling, to me, but still true, when I thought of all the messages sent for me in this lifetime, and read about the messages to those who have met trouble, too.

Why bother with these ideas which others think are nothing but random thoughts? Seems to me that the better we practice and understand pure thought, the easier we can talk with other aspects of ourselves and others, on their many levels. Can we practice speaking back? Will they respond? Maybe it's just fun.

And maybe my pleasure is languages, the rivers that join souls and spirits and mortals together. Is there someone in this little family who hears from time to time and maybe speaks these languages, too?

I think that could be true.

*O*ur Silent Fires

*I*T HAPPENED IN the state of Iowa, and when it struck, I happened to be mowing the lawn. The back yard of the rented house was at the edge of town, on the hillside. Leafy summertime, and from the yard one could see other hillsides, trees in the sunlight, to the horizon.

Could I have been pushing a hand mower or was there a gasoline engine on the machine? I think it must have had the engine, I think there were heavy waves of loud that afternoon. Back and forth . . . zoom . . . zoom in the middle of the 1960's. *Jonathan Seagull* was an unfinished manuscript, forgotten at the bottom of a stack of other manuscripts.

Zoom . . . sometimes slowing in the thickest grass. How am

I going to finish this lifetime, I thought. So many expenses, so little income from the few books. I didn't know why I was here, right when I was facing . . . what? When you've got no money in a culture that needs money to live. I didn't think of it as a divine test for mortals, then. It was the leading edge of disaster.

Why did I bother to mow the lawn? What can I do that will somehow stop the sound of destruction for this life? Could I get a job at the airport? Would a business there want me for an instructor? Some up times, as a writer, some down ones with other jobs. Will it always be up and down, hills like this lawn, trying to live day after day?

At least I was mowing the lawn. I turned the mower around at the high side of the lawn. A little distance below was a barbed-wire fence where there used to be cows, more hills, and the horizon. When I turned, I looked up for a second and the trees were on fire!

I stopped, I couldn't believe! All of them! The shapes of the trees, near-trees and horizon-trees, were swept in waves of bright orange, shimmering sunrise colors, splashes of sudden blues changing second to second. The barbed wire was glowing, as if it was electricity, pulsing the same fires as the trees.

For some reason I didn't scream and run. I stood there, unmoving, and looked. I didn't think *what's going on?* Didn't think at all. Just soaked in the colors of the trees, the grass, the fence wires, the firestorm of colors, for half a minute. Then the fire settled down, the fireworks slower, smaller, the wire cooling until it was old wire again, and then the trees were just trees, everyday trees, green leaves and shadows in the afternoon.

After a long stunned minute, I closed my mouth and finished mowing the yard. I had no idea what had happened or what it was supposed to mean. What could I have said: "I saw the world burn up, but it's fine now?"

Life went on. I was a flight instructor for a while, wrote articles at night for magazines. Step by step. There's a reason. I don't know what the reason is, I thought, so I might as well keep living until I learn why.

A while later, weeks, months, years later, I remembered the fires. One clue: they weren't fires — they were auras! We all have auras we can't see (well, some people see them). Do trees have auras? Later I heard about Kirlian photographs. Close but not the forest on fire, and the glowing barbed wire.

It's never happened since. One half-minute in one lifetime.

Why?

In the Bible, the story about the burning bush that was not consumed, that was the same thing that I saw. Not a bush, though, a whole forest, horizon to horizon, afire for thirty seconds while I stood there, mowing the lawn. Was it whispering, *This world is not what you think it is!*

As far as I know, I haven't written about that strange scene. It's been locked in my mind all these years, and when I woke this morning I saw some trees out the window and they reminded me. They didn't catch fire, they were just quiet little trees. Yet I thought, behind the everydayness of the trees, do their auras sweep upward like flames around them all? Do the fires of our own auras, I wondered, do they lift and fall as we live our screenplays, as we trace our beliefs on the world we chose for our lessons?

What lovely silent fires we light, never seeing them, as we play!

*H*ow Do I . . .

OME QUESTIONS FROM a friend. "How do you just quit being jealous? How do you just quit being angry? "

It took me just forty years to quit. I found that when I was left by one I loved, or when I was angry, the same thing happened in my mind, always the same words: *You're frightened. You're going to lose something! Protect it!*

After slipping into protecting without thinking, decade after decade, I decided that I didn't like feeling jealousy and anger. Finally I asked, feeling helpless, "*Well, what am I going to lose?*

"I'll lose her, is what!" I said.

"Oh?" Another voice in my mind, my high spiritual self. "Can you answer my questions?"

"Of course I'll answer. I'm jealous and angry, but I'll answer if you don't require a page to listen."

"Three questions."

"You can take ten, but three is a third better."

"Thank you," and it paused. "*Do you love her?*"

"Silly spirit! Of course I love her. I wouldn't be with her if I . . ."

"You don't have to explain. The answer is enough. Next question. *Do you want her to be happy?*"

"Sill . . . yes! I want her to be . . ."

"*Third question: Do you trust her to make her own decisions about her happiness?*"

A short silence. "I do."

Long silence.

"What?" I said.

"Are you jealous now?"

I love her, I thought. I want her to be happy. Of course I trust her to make her own decisions.

Highspeed thinking:

If I don't love her, I can be jealous (but why would I want to be with her if I didn't love her?).

If I don't want her to be happy I can be jealous (but do I want her to stay with me when I don't want her happy?).

If I don't trust her, I can be jealous (but why would I want to love someone whose choices I don't like?).

"Well, of course I'm still . . ." Where was that feeling that was twisting my heart? ". . . well, of course . . ." It was gone! "What did you do with my jeal . . . Oh. Thank you."

Three questions my spirit self had asked. Any "No" told me that I didn't want to be close to one I thought I loved. All Yesses told me whatever she decides to do about her happiness is what I want for her, too. If I'm happy for her to be with another guy, and she can be with me when she wants to be.

(Historical footnote: I found in my heart, that I didn't really like all her choices. Jealousy gone. Romantic relationship gone.)

Those three questions have worked for me: one, two, three; ever since. No jealousy since.

Anger? Can one just decide not to be angry? Can one decide not to be afraid? Isn't anger always fear? If I'm not frightened, I cannot be angry. Same question the minute a conflict arises: *I'm afraid! I'm going to lose something! Protect it!*

How do I protect, I said, what do I do . . .

"Don't do anything," said the spirit. "We *do* without a word, no fear, no anger required. You can disappear, you can resist, you can choose swords, all those choices so calm. But for anger, for fear, you need words."

Words. "Without words, I'll lose this discussion, the argument," my protoanger self said, "and everyone will think he won! And don't you see? He's saying that he's right about evil spirits and I know there's no such thing . . . he'll win unless I say something aggressive and powerful!"

"*What am I going to lose?*" the spirit said. "Nothing. An argument doesn't prevail in words, it prevails in your own inner decisions."

How had I been dragged into a land of words, I thought, a place I had no reason to be! Move to my own land:

"You may be right." And all at once there was nothing to be angry about. He may be right. Not in my heart, but in his.

"Richard," the spirit tested me. "What if he says, 'You're a prince of the devil, you're a demon, because . . .'"

Stay on my own land.

"Could be," I said. "I could be a demon." No anger, a smile instead.

"Now he can say anything, he can say, 'And you're the Antichrist!'"

"Maybe so." Words. When someone wants to win, let them

win. I have my own ideas, others have theirs. I don't need to convince anyone that what they think or what I think is right or it's wrong.

When the Internet happened, there were words in long-term print, some true, some not . . . truths and lies. It was the same for me, just the same as for everyone chatted about on the Web. What makes me think words told about me have to be true? It could be, from the printed words in Google, that the President of the United States is an alien, a reptilian from outer space. Well, why can't I be an alien from the Pleiades or a daisy from the meadow? I don't have to be angry for the President, or for me. Anything could be true, in other minds.

"So what if someone appears in my home out of the dark," said my never-want-to-lose mortal mind, "and plans to kill me and my loved one and my puppy? Should I not be angry?"

"No anger required. No words, only action for the intruder," said my advanced spiritual inner spirit, which I guess knows everything. "Just shoot 'im."

*A*m I Getting Smarter?

*O*R ARE THE THINGS IN this life a lot simpler than they once seemed? Does simplicity come from a few old words used in a new way?

By the blessing of my airplane crash, I've learned that "death" at the end of our Earth-time is not death at all, it is a beautiful new Life.

After letting go of events so familiar, at once the colors are brighter and scenes are different from ever on Earth. There are no evils around, we find friends that we've known ever, we don't have to struggle to live. Coming back to Life again, with its teachers and guides for us and for our friends, most of us gradually getting better at Earthlife, suddenly we can see what once we called a "lifetime" isn't a lifetime at all. It was just one act in our cosmic screenplay.

All at once we understand why we lived that role, we see the lessons we hoped to show during our Earthtime. What we called our lifetime is "Act 12" or "Act 2431," and all of our acts become the Play as it seems to us. Act after act, lesson after lesson, triumphs and not-quite-rights and shoot-it-overs.

Out of the play for a while when we "die," we can rest as long as we wish, do nothing, imagine and choose lifestories yet to be in our acts, including some that are most likely impossible. We can play any role of any of our beliefs, any time we wish, several at once, if that suits us.

I remember the ending of one act that happened when I (writing this, today) was only three years old. In 1939, I was unaware that the pilot who was me in his scene of the play was 19 years old. He was chased by an enemy aircraft, spiraled down to escape, and turned his airplane all the way into the sea. I remembered just that part of his lifetime, the ending, four decades later. I saw the sea rising up, so close to the windscreen, and the next frame I saw from a hundred meters away, the crash, the tower of spray and the airplane gone.

"So what?" Good question. Maybe it's "Nothing," for others. For me, I began to know why I have the tests I do in this act, this lifetime. I can tell which I did well in former scenes, and which tests that come for me now because I didn't quite master them when I tried last time.

Alcohol, tobacco, drugs . . . all simple in this scene for me, I think I learned from tests before. For me, just the suggestion of Alcohol Etc. means disaster for me, a coiled snake ready to strike. Did I have a single event in this lifetime with them? Thanks to the snake, not one test, not one challenge here. Somewhere long ago I learned they're losers, first sight.

Loneliness? I may finally have learned in this act, a major test. I'm still playing.

Age? It goes on. I guess I'll find out later.

Medicine? Either an F or an A. I know nothing of medicine, had a bunch of medical things thrust on me after my crash in this scene. I decided not to fight about it.

Anger? It was a test till I knew I don't have to play with it, ever. I just quit being angry.

Patience? Maybe some progress, but between thee and me, I think I haven't learned that lesson yet.

Love? The big test in my play. Quite a few failures, for me, and perhaps one win. Strange, but I think a win.

Average? Maybe a C+, over all, for this act.

How can we earn an A? So simple. So difficult. Remember, when the scene comes with its test: We are each a perfect expression of perfect Love, no matter what seems to be—through every act, through every scene along our thousand-year play.

*R*arely Asked Questions: How did Jonathan Seagull come to you?

*N*OT THE WAY I expected it to come.

The first time in my life I heard a voice, with no one there to speak it. I was walking alone one evening, a starving young writer desperate to know how I was going to pay the rent. Then someone behind me and to my right, said, "Jonathan Livingston Seagull." It was decades before I realized that was a simple, honest answer to my question.

I turned, pretty well startled, and there was no one there. I went home, frightened, and locked the door behind me, wondering who was the voice and what was a Jonathan Livingston Seagull. Hours of puzzlement later, about the time I had to admit I hadn't a clue what was a Jonathan

Livingston Seagull, my office wall disappeared, and in its place, a Cinerama screen. On the screen I saw the ocean below, and the sky and one solitary that's what must be a Jonathan Seagull.

The story unfolded and I wrote what I saw, as fast as I could write, scene by scene.

Two thirds of the way through Part I some discarnate apparently tripped over the Cinerama power cord and the movie disappeared, turned back into a wall again.

I liked the little guy I had met, liked him at once, but I had no idea how to finish his story. He has these different ideas, he does this crazy flying, he's thrown out of his Flock *and then what?* Not one single idea of then-what. Couldn't finish the story.

Eight years later, 1500 miles away, I woke from a dream with *that's then-what!* I flew out of bed, typed as fast as I could type till it was finished.

Part 2 and 3 followed, no movies required since I had learned in those years to trust my imaginings.

Any story that comes in this strange way, I thought, is destined for instant success with readers. What happened is that *Jonathan Livingston Seagull* was instantly rejected for publication, then rejected again, and again . . . rejected 18 times before my agent sent the manuscript back to me. "I like your story, Richard, but nobody in Manhattan can stand it. Time to put it away and go on to your next book."

In that same mail with that final rejection was one other

letter. From an editor at Macmillan Publishing Company: "Dear Richard Bach I've read some of your work and find it interesting. Would you happen to have a manuscript that is not committed to another publisher? If so, I would love to . . ."

The manuscript went back to New York at the speed of light, Eleanor Friede loved what she read, even though another editor at Macmillan had already rejected the story.

Then it turned out that my friend Russell Munson, pilot and professional photographer just happened to have hundreds of photos he had taken, years earlier, when for no particular reason he had felt like taking pictures of seagulls.

The photos matched the text perfectly, even that impossible shot: "His feathers ruffled, he stalled and fell." I didn't know that seagull feathers ruffle when their wings stall, except for seeing it in that psychic movie. Russell got the proof that they do.

First printing was 5,000 copies. Something like 40 million copies have sold around the world to date. If you have a first edition, these days, I will be happy to buy it for, say, twice the cover price . . .

*R*arely Asked Questions: How I started flying . . .

I LEARNED TO fly airplanes because I took a course in archery, my only year in college.

At the archery range, the man next to me, instead of firing his arrow, relaxed his bow and looked up at a little airplane flying overhead.

How strange, I thought . . . nobody looks at airplanes unless they have a special interest in them. So by way of a joke, I said, "I'll bet you're looking for someone to come out to the airport every weekend, wash and polish your airplane and if they do that you'll teach them how to fly." Just that crazy sentence popped into my head.

Bob Keech turned to me a little startled and said, "How did you know?"

He had just earned his Limited Flight Instructor certificate, and needed to train five student pilots before he could become a real Certified Flight Instructor. And there I stood, Student Number One.

I washed and polished his Luscombe 8E, had my first flying lessons and soloed. I loved it, went crazy for flying, dropped out of college, joined the Air Force as an Aviation Cadet, never looked back.

How our lives are shaped by impossible coincidence!

Famous Quotes I Didn't Write

*H*OW I'D LOVE to take credit for some of the grand thoughtful sayings orbiting the Internet that somehow got warranted to me! How I not-love getting credit for some of the others quotes I can't believe are true.

****

I don't want to do business with those who don't make a profit, because they can't give the best service.
—Richard Bach

Never heard of this line, and I don't much care whether any business (besides mine) makes a profit or gives the best service. Most likely said by a different Richard Bach, of whom there are many. Some of them get mail for me, and once in a while I get mail for them.

****

A professional writer is an amateur who didn't quit.
—Richard Bach

Bright clear insight, and true . . . every professional writer was once an amateur, no guarantee they'd survive. I've quoted that line at talks I've given, said it was from Samuel Johnson. Then I had a doubt about that, as it sounds a little modern for Sam. According to Google, the person who said it was . . . me! I didn't write it. Who did? Please don't say it doesn't matter, or the custom of attributing quotes to somebody even when they're not the source will collapse. Let me know when you find who said it first.

****

If you love someone, set them free. If they come back they're yours; if they don't they never were. —Richard Bach

A fine sentiment. Not mine, unfortunately.

****

In order to win, you must expect to win. —Richard Bach

Not true. I've won now and then when I didn't expect, and lost sometimes when I expected otherwise. As I wouldn't bet the farm on this one, I decided not to write it.

****

It is by not always thinking of yourself, if you can manage it, that you might somehow be happy. Until you make room in your life for someone as important to you as yourself, you will always be searching and lost. — Richard Bach

A new category: from a book of mine, but not said by me. That's Leslie Parrish speaking, in *The Bridge Across Forever*.

****

Our soulmate is the one who makes life come to life. —*Richard Bach*

That's Leslie's, too.

****

Strong beliefs win strong men, and then make them stronger.
— Richard Bach

Not a clue, who said that.

****

The simplest things are often the truest.
— Richard Bach

This one has a vague resemblance to something I wrote. But it's tumbled so far downstream, shedding parts along the way, that it'd take a while to find the original.

****

No matter how qualified or deserving we are, we will never reach a better life
until we can imagine it for ourselves and allow ourselves to have it.
— Richard Bach

Sounds sort of like me, but not.

****

When you have come to the edge of all the light you have
And step into the darkness of the unknown
Believe that one of the two will happen to you
Either you'll find something solid to stand on
Or you'll be taught how to fly! *— Richard Bach*

Grand inspiring quote. Wish I had written it.

****

What matters most: What he had yearned to embrace was not the flesh but a downy spirit, a spark, the impalpable angel that inhabits the flesh. Wind, Sand and Stars. — Richard Bach

This may be one of those rare fell-into-the-blender quotes. Some nice idea from somebody (Antoine de Saint-Exupery, who wrote *Wind, Sand and Stars*?), not moi.

****

If you love someone, set them free. If they come back they're yours; if they don't they never were. —Richard Bach

It's not just once, you're misquoted, it's over and over and over again.

****

You are never given a dream without also being given the power to make it true. You may have to work for it, however. — Richard Bach

A not-quite quote. 'Tisn't "dream," but "wish."

****

You are never given a wish without what it takes to make it true.
—Richard Bach

At least they got the "wish" part right.

****

Everybody is given a Dream . . . you may have to work for it however . . .
—Richard Bach

At least they got the "work for it" part right.

****

Moćna ideja je apsolutno fantastična i potpuno beskorisna ako ne odlučimo da je ostvarimo.

Gar khodavand cheshm dar cheshmat nahad va gooyad: farmanat daham ta zende'ee be shadi dar in jahan sar koni. Che khahi kard?

Ένας επαγγελματίας συγγραφέας είναι ένας ερασιτέχνης που δεν τα παράτησε.

Може ли разстоянието наистина да те раздели от приятелите ти . . .
Ако искаш да си с някого, когото обичаш, не си ли вече там при него?
—Richard Bach

I love languages. I hope these words are mine.

****

Whatever harm I would do to another, I shall do first to myself.
As I respect and am kind to myself, so shall I respect and be kind to peers, to elders, to kits.
I claim for others the freedom to live as they wish, to think and believe as they will. I claim that freedom for myself.
I shall make each choice and live each day to my highest sense of right.
—Richard Bach

Hurray! A spot-on accurate quote from *The Ferret Chronicles!*
Someone has read my ferret books! Freeze frame on the Los

186

Angeles freeway at rush hour, say, "Honk if you've read *The Ferret Chronicles*," and you will hear absolute silence.

One voice, defiant: "I love those stories anyway!"—that's a quote from me.

*Q*uiz for Pilots

*H*ERE'S A judgment-test for you. Don't be concerned, it's just a little quiz, and of course our lives depend on your decision:

It's early April. You and I are flying the Lake Amphibian from Florida to Washington State, westbound out of Rawlins, Wyoming at noon toward Twin Falls, Idaho. It was summer in Florida, but right now we're 30 miles east of Ogden and the outside air temperature is 12 degrees F. I'd like to turn the heater on, but I haven't run it since last winter and if some bird built a nest in there we'll have a fire when I hit the Heater-Start switch and I'm not up to a fire just now I'd rather freeze.

We're cruising at 10,500 feet, about as high as the Lake can go ... we might make 11,500 with takeoff rpm, still air and a lot of patience. Wind is 14 knots from the west.

The weather was supposed to be clear ahead, but by the time we got here it looks like ... well, it's what we see in the photo. The ceiling at Logan, off to the north, is 2,000 feet broken to overcast.

So look ahead for a bit and then I'll turn to you. "What do you think?"

You frown. "Hm. Up or down."

Sure enough, we can climb above the undercast ahead, cruise right on over the mountains, let down northwest of Ogden and make it to Twin Falls. But what if there are no holes in the undercast when we get northwest of Ogden? Neither one of us is instrument-current so there's no descending-through-clouds for us.

Or we could go down beneath the cloud deck, try it that way. You can see the visibility's not so good underneath. The terrain runs around 7,000 feet . . . If the bases are at 9,000, there'll be not a whole lot of room between us and the clouds above, between us and the rocks below. Not many places to land if the engine stops.

Nearest airport is Evanston, behind us now. It's open.

We can divert now and make it back to Evanston, but there's only 20 miles of rough country ahead.   If we make it, the pass at Ogden, it's smooth sailing all the way to Seattle.

Fly high, most likely there's a hole on the other side. What if we get downdrafts . . . we're right at our service ceiling and a downdraft drags us helpless clawing down a thousand feet a minute. What if the engine fails when we're on top over all that rugged land, waiting hard and patient under the cloud? Do you relish gliding down on instruments, everything's fog outside, wondering whether we'll break out with enough altitude to pick some place to land or will it be rocks we see mid-cloud, a half-second before we hit?

And look at that . . . the GPS just failed! Of all the times for the thing to quit . . .

We've got a paper map.   And we ought to be right about . . . here's this little river . . .

"Let's take it down."

Go down low, and try for it? I agree.

Remarkable, the way flying clears the mind!

So down we go, and sure enough the visibility drops to three miles, a little less. There the peaks are jutting snow up to the clouds. Map says that one's at 7,760, that one's at 8,767 and it's into the overcast. No sight of human life below, no ranches, no roads, no nothin'. Engine quits now we can land wheels-up in the snow, but we'll never take off again in this high country.

One more ridge in front of us, clear it and we'll be able to drop down a little lower. Leave room for a 180-degree turn if it goes to fog ahead of us, nice easy turn in thin air. Visibility's going down.

Only fifteen miles to go! So close! Turn back now to Evanston, or press on?

You think we can clear that ridge, just squeak over it? And what if the weather's worse on the other side, it closes down to the ridge-top behind us? Then we're forced to go on instruments, climb as best we can through the clag, hope to break out on top?

She's a close call, this one. What's your choice?

— End of quiz —

Here's the terrain, on a map that doesn't show clouds, snow, turbulence, downdrafts:

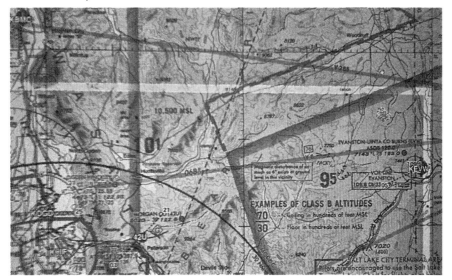

Soon as you disappeared from the cockpit, I made my decision. I turned back to Evanston. It was snowing when the wheels touched the runway.

Some wise pilot once told me, "I like to ask myself about my dumb ideas, 'How will it look on the accident report?'"

We probably would have made it, of course, flying low. Weather probably would have been fine. But would I bet my life on it, would I bet yours? Say we cleared that ridge, and the weather was worse on the other side, and if in the middle of some downdraft trying to climb through the clouds we ran our airplane into some granite cliffside—the report would say that I chose to do that, chose to risk our lives for the sake of a few miles and a few hours. Not a good-lookin' document.

Next day the weather was better, a fading reminder of yesterday's storms.

My video of that flight is all iPhone amateur, and just long enough to suggest that we're up there for more than a hundredth of a second, when we're flying, we're in the air minute after minute, hour by hour.

The sound's amateur, too, but perhaps you can hear what "faithful engine" sounds like, purring on over jagged land. It helps imagine how pilots come to love their machines.

Bonus question:

```
            KRWL, Rawlins Muni/Harvey Field
                VFR, 84nm E, DA=8,190'
KRWL 081753Z AUTO 21033G43KT 10SM CLR 51F/23F A2964

          KEVW, Evanston-Uinta County Burns Field
                IFR, 90nm W, DA=7,291'
KEVW 081824Z AUTO 33004KT 2SM -SN BR SCT004 OVC011
30F/28F A2960
```

Would you prefer to land at Rawlins or Evanston? :)

Note: This is not a color book. Imagine that the scarf I'm wearing is striped in bright lemon and delicious flame colors.

M y Scarf

Y OU CAN TELL I'm proud of this scarf.

It was presented to me by Bethany Ferret, captain of the Ferret Rescue Vessel *Resolute,* a gift after *Rescue Ferrets at Sea* was published.

Those are the colors and stripes of *Resolute* and its crew, in one of my favorite stories of all I've written.

The book is out of print, at least for now, but the story's there in *Curious Lives*, along with four others that touched and changed, helped me along my path to becoming human.

I'm one of two from the outside world who've received the

honor, the other is Chloe Ferret, the journalist and rock star. Of course I'm proud!

*B*ooks I Read, Movies I Watch, Over and Over

*Y*OU CAN TELL a lot about a person when you know what she loves to read, what he loves to watch. What's a really private guy doing with a website in which he chooses to show these to whomever drops by? Is a puzzlement. (You're remembering that line from *The King and I*, aren't you?) Perhaps he cares more about being known to his little family around the world, reflecting their own values, than he does about his online privacy.

Why, paint me unsophisticated! These lists will keep grow-ing, snap-peas on vines. Like peas, no particular order. At first I had a line about why I like each one. Then I figured if you read the book or saw the movie, you'd know why. You'll notice not a single horror film here, or raunchy comedy, being as how I'm into neither raunch nor horror. Music? Hopelessly old-fashioned, wildly romantic. Beethoven's Ninth, Holst's Planets (and therefore John Williams score for *Star Wars*), close harmonies as in the Four Freshmen (who started it all), the Association, the Beach Boys, the Mamas and the Papas. I know, hopeless. *Duelin' Banjos*, of course.

Television I turned off forever on September 11, 2001. I do not miss it. Get my news from the Internet.

Books by Other Writers:

- *Dandelion Wine*, by Ray Bradbury
- *Fahrenheit 451*, by Ray Bradbury

- *The Fountainhead*, by Ayn Rand
- *Man and Time*, by J. B. Priestly
- *You Were Born Again to be Together*, by Dick Sutphen
- *Atlas Shrugged*, by Ayn Rand
- *The Dancing Wu Li Masters*, by Gary Zukov
- *The Tao of Physics*, by Fritjof Capra
- *Stalking the Wild Pendulum*, by Itzhak Bentov
- *The Nature of Personal Reality*, by Jane Roberts
- *Seth Speaks*, by Jane Roberts
- *Trustee from the Toolroom*, by Nevil Shute
- *An Experiment with Time*, by J. W. Dunne
- *The Rainbow and the Rose*, by Nevil Shute
- *Round the Bend*, by Nevil Shute
- *Secrets of a Buccaneer-Scholar*, by James Bach
- *Life After Life*, by Raymond Moody
- *Breakthrough to Creativity*, by Shafica Karagulla
- *The Act of Creation*, by Arthur Koestler
- *Psychical Phenonomena in the Physical World*, by Charles Mc-Creery
- *The Mysterious Island*, by Jules Verne
- *20,000 Leagues Under the Sea*, by Jules Verne
- *Captain Stormfield's Visit to Heaven*, by Mark Twain
- *Beautiful Joe's Paradise*, by Mashall Saunders (that's a Ms. Marshall Saunders)
- *The Flying Yorkshireman*, by Eric Knight
- *As a Man Thinketh*, by James Allen
- *In Search of Schroedinger's Cat*, by John Gribbin
- *Language in Thought and Action*, by S. I. Hayakawa
- *The Supreme Adventure*, by Robert Crookall
- *Wind, Sand and Stars*, by Antoine de Saint-Exupery
- *Flight to Arras*, by Antoine de Saint-Exupery
- *Night Flight*, by Antoine de Saint-Exupery
- *The Holographic Universe*, by Michael Talbot
- *Education and Ecstasy*, by George Leonard

Movies:

- *GalaxyQuest*
- *Enchanted April*
- *Heaven Can Wait*
- *Mouse Hunt*
- *Chicken Run*
- *The Princess Bride*
- *The Scarlet Pimpernel (Anthony Andrews, Jane Seymour)*
- *Sense and Sensibility*
- *The Electric Horseman*
- *Bell, Book and Candle*
- *Somewhere in Time*
- *A Christmas Carol (Alastair Sim as Scrooge)*
- *Always*
- *Nine to Five*
- *The Hunters (because I flew some of those very F-86's and once with James Salter, the author of the book)*
- *True Lies*
- *Shaun the Sheep*
- *All the President's Men*
- *Harold and Maude*
- *Groundhog Day*
- *Men in Black*
- *Creature Comforts (Nick Park claymation)*
- *Butch Cassidy and the Sundance Kid*
- *Horatio Hornblower (Series)*
- *My Fair Lady*
- *Ordinary People*
- *Remains of the Day*
- *Strictly Ballroom*
- *The Court Jester*
- *Casablanca*
- *Finding Nemo*
- *Avatar*
- *The Sting*

- *Searching for Bobby Fischer*
- *It's a Wonderful Life*

I Didn't Dream This, Did I?

SOMEONE, NO POINT IN SAYING WHO, wrote a message to me two or three days ago, about the ExtraTerrestial chapter that I put on the website.

She wrote and said that the ETs would enjoy the chance to talk with me. My Ferret Chronicle books taught me to be courteous to practically anyone. "That's a kind thought," I wrote back to her. "I'd like to talk with them, too. Would you care to tell me who they are?"

She did, next message. She said that she had a recent connection to the Sirian B extraterrestials, the Arcturians, and Pleiadians and that she has spoken for years with angelic and some spirit guides, too. She's a lightworker. She mentioned that she was connected with a group called the Ascension Alliance. She's a medium (of course), she listens to them and translates their thoughts into to our language.

What would you have done, with an email like this? Yes. I did, that too. I went on the Internet to read about the Ascension Alliance, and found that they're a religious group, there are rites and an organization of apparently wise people, they wear white robes . . .

So reading this, I replied that I appreciated her messages, but I have a little problem with religious organizations, and I would not be talking with the AA, that she must have mistranslated the name they said, but it wasn't me.

Kind as I could be, I thought that was the end of the correspondence. Except on the next mail she said, "I think your Internet research connection switched to a different organization. The AA is not a religious group. They are simply ETs and spiritual beings who care about us."

So I wrote back, said something of the principles that I value: not only that the most powerful, but the only reality is Love, I said. Everything else, this world of space-time and every other one designed on limits is an illusion, a dream that we come to from our after-world illusion, when we feel like testing our certainty of Love no matter what images dance before us. We'll see injustice and death and deliberate lies planned to enrich some people, we'll see joy and laughter and love there, too.

I'm afraid I went on for a while, since these ideas do not often make sense to others who believe that the power is God, not

Love, and that this world has a lot of uncomfortable reality on it, and a lot of things we don't understand.

That should have chased her away. But you know what she did. The next message in my mailbox, it was her again. "That's why the ETs want to talk with you. They've been watching you for years, and now it's time to talk."

So I asked her how I talk with them. Would she be the interpreter?

No, she said, next message. There was a place that I could imagine when I was meditating from a quiet gentle frame of mind. I was to go there, and see what would happen. That was it.

I simply had to put my new book down for a while and try this. OK, I thought. I can do this.

So before I went to sleep, I relaxed my body, relaxed my mind, felt free of the chains of this world. Body asleep, mind alert, I imagined moving to where she had said to be.

There they were. I don't remember their faces, just the same as a Near Death Experience – we see others, but most often not clearly.   Instead of thinking that they would be doing something with me, I asked them a few questions:

"Why are you all here on our planet? What do you want from us?"

They didn't use words, which is common through all the books about them I've read, and about spirits. They use telepathy which I hear as ideas in good English.

"We're here because we're your family!"

I have a small recognition of family, as we're a kind of family, here on this website. But the family includes angels and guides and ETs from light-years away? That was a startlement, and it made perfect sense the second I heard it. It still makes sense to me now. I love the idea of an exoplanetary family.

"If you're spiritual beings, though," I said, "why do the ETs use spaceships and UFOs, to reach us? Why do you appear and disappear in some fifth dimension, where we can't follow?"

"Of course you can follow," they said, "you will when you learn to do it. You're a young culture, and if you don't blow your beautiful planet into tiny little pieces, you'll learn to do a lot more than fifth dimension travel.

"Why do we use UFO's? Because we need you to become interested, become curious about us. Have you noticed how often you hear stories about us these days, when fifty years ago there was nothing? Have you noticed that no matter how the governments say we don't exist, that we do, anyway?" There was a quiet for a minute while I thought about that.

"You know, don't you, that if we wanted to destroy you, at least some of us would have done that thousands of years ago. But we don't care for destroying things. We love your curiosity, your creativity, the wonder of your imaginations. Even though some of you are frightened of us, you don't need to be." Another silence.

"We're concerned with the everpresent wars that your

206

leaders are beginning now and that your children obey. Bigger wars, lasting not against a defined enemy, but against empty words: terrorism, religions, imagined destroyers. Just one nuclear mistake, and you'll be gone, with your art and sciences and part of our family in this belief of space and time. Of course your spirits cannot die any more than we can, you'll appear as other creatures on other planets for a while, till you discover you don't need the limits of physical bodies.

"But perhaps we could make one simple introduction soon . . . a thousand ET spaceships, as you once said, hovering over every capital cities of your planet. We wouldn't do anything, destroy anything, hurt anyone. We'd just be there, and hope you'd realize that your family is spread across the stars, and welcomes you to reach up and meet us."

All these words, please forgive me, but they said that in just a second and I had to write it down in American English.

They let me play with bi-locating, which was a lot easier than I thought it would be. Impossible for me now, of course, but when I was there, I could be flying a saucer way overhead, yet still be standing in the midst of them . . . it was easy.

Then my time with them was over. I needed to spend hours thinking about this. I'm still thinking about it.

Was the meeting with the angels (who said nothing) and ETs (who said all this) a dream?

It didn't feel like a dream. I was resting in bed, my body unmoving, but my mind as alert as it is when I'm flying.

Am I crazy? No more than usual.

I'll probably try to reach them again. What matters now, is this: Does this little adventure mean anything to you? Did they reach me because it was a way they could reach you?

I have no idea.

*W*hy Are *We Here?*

*T*HE LONGER WE spend wondering, the more easily answers come. The reason why we're here, I've just discovered, is written not in some book of magic, it's written in our daily lives.

Pretend, for a minute, that we've all come to Earth to learn something. Since we may not care for little boxy classrooms, instead we have a whole planet for our current lessons. Now pretend that there's not one of us navigated into this belief of life on the planet, including thee and me, who isn't in the test of some major challenge.

For our lessons to matter for us, to make a forever comment in our infinite experience of life, we must pretend that this world spins in a river of amnesia, no past for us to remember, from the day we're born. We must have a physical body with lots of limitations: no unaided flying, no shape-shifting spirits, no telepathy, no connection with friends of different lifetimes. We must believe that this act in our play is real, that it's not a scene we've chosen to play.

Some of our lessons are easy (How shall I be kind to someone who loves me?). Some of them may take a while (Why did my little airplane lack four inches of altitude above the high-tension wires and therefore she crashed inverted into the ground?). Others are difficult (Why did my daughter die in a snowy head-on car collision one minute after she decided to unfasten her seat belt?).

It's an early belief for most of us, at the start, that we're helpless pawns in a vast uncaring universe. We think that we have to eat to live, find some shelter, protect ourselves from hungry animals and raiding humans, dodge volcanoes, duck under asteroids on a collision with our planet, and by the way, if we're curious in our spare time, find a meaning for it all. We believe that consciousness has nothing to do with the world around us. Physical things, we're told, are real.

When we begin to understand, from near-death experience, from teachers we admire, from our intuition, that we're eternal souls, and that no disaster can happen in any of our pretend play-lives to touch our highest self . . . that's our lesson! Done! A-plus!

That's why we're here.

The number of categories in our lessons is infinite. What if we're poor, or what if we're rich? What do we do with the appearances? What if we're plain like me, or beautiful? When if we don't care to have lessons, or if we do care? What about our belief of illnesses, of dangers of living, dangers of working, what if we don't love what we're doing, what if we do? What if we love someone who doesn't love us back, or what if she / he does love us back? What if we love alcohol and drugs? What if we believe we need medicines? What if there are no doctors in our lives, and what if there are? What if we're bored with life? What if we want to die, how do we do that? What if we decide not to kill ourselves?

Relationships, other people, ourselves, sports, love and hatred, blocks in our wishes. different paths appearing suddenly or slowly, what if friends die, schools and teachers end, what do we do about ideas which we love and the ones we disagree with; is television necessary, movies, governments? There are tests for us in everything. Sometimes death appears to be the mark of a failure, sometimes death is a beautiful success.

Take your pencil and name two tests you're working with now. Don't list a hundred, just two you're having. Your answers to them determine the quality of your spirit, at this moment.

What are my tests, you ask? Loneliness, for one. For two, my belief that I've already lived too long in this act. I sense that if I give up on either, I'll probably decide to take the tests again.

The lesson for us all: What's more powerful than our belief of death? Answer: Love is. And: We are!

And finally, a truth for why we're here that takes years for us to discover, right in the midst of all the stories that space and time may offer for us to believe:

We are perfect expressions of perfect Love, right here, right now.

*I*s Perfection Too Much To Ask?

I NEVER THOUGHT SO. Seems to work for everyone who decides to live with another human being. Works for every marriage.

When one decides for marriage, they're done with dating, at last; they've found the single person who mirrors their own perfections, and they're off on tests and challenges and beautiful understandings that only a life with a lovely human being can offer. The odds against that are barely this side of impossible, yet it happens time and time again, to millions and millions of us.

What makes it work, I think, is the magic of intimacy. There is one person with whom we can talk about anything, we can splash our imaginations, we can build events that won't work, but still our dear ones love us. Without intimacy, some say, what's the point of living? Without magic there are clouds to muffle every sunrise.

I think now that perfections are easier to find when we're young. We haven't learned what doesn't work, we're free to design any relationship that makes us smile, and then go ahead and live it. If it doesn't quite work, we put it on the Experience page of our ledger, and gradually become comfortable with the life we've always wanted.

All the lovely things that blossom for us, the ones we share with our intimate friend, make the life we most enjoy. By the time we've lived for a while, we know what we want from our days, and what we know will be a loss. Gradually we become perfect at being us.

I look at myself, critically. Am I perfect? Basically, of course I am. I have discovered my can'ts and joys. Can't: No smoking, no drinking, no birthdays, no television, no anger, I invite no one that I don't admire in my house.

Joys: Beauty, just about endless solitude with a perfect Other, laughter, quiet talks about the ways we think, startling events that have touched each of us. Teaching each other all we've learned. Courtesy. Flying, of course. And a puppy.

Since I stopped memorializing birthdays when I was 16 or so, I have no idea how old I am. I must be 80 or 90.

Which is why I found that perfection on being us tends to keep us alone, unless we've been married for a long time. Our can'ts shut down others we might have loved as teenagers. Some lovely person lights a cigarette (killed my mom) or drinks a cocktail (killed a friend), I'm hoping I can leave quickly. I'm too courteous to offend an innocent person, but I want to leave.

There was a dinner a friend suggested years ago. He suggested a day when all the filming on a movie would be finished, a sort of celebration. Sounded good. He and I and two young women. Yet in the middle of the meal the subjects of talk were somehow difficult for me (I don't remember what I don't like) and I thought for a minute and finally said, "I don't think my mind is here, and I don't think my body should be here either." Their looks said What? I paid for the meal with the waitress, and left.

In one way that was a perfect moment. In another, it was insufferable.

If that was years ago, have I mentioned how difficult I must be for the few friends who still care for me?

What all this means, for me and for others who have crafted their perfections, is we get used to living by ourselves. In time, there are so many events that matter to us, that we won't give them up for a new relationship. We'd love the intimacy, but the Other won't trade her sport-fishing for an airplane, or her comfortable apartment for a place alone on a mountaintop, no matter how beautiful is the view. No one is ready to shift into mine as I am not willing to shift into theirs.

One learns this by 90 or so. There's a reason why living long means living lonely. I'm responsible for every event that's changed my life into what it is now. Thank you, Richard, I think.

For the first time in my life, I've quit. I am not looking for this amazing woman who must be somewhere but I don't know how to reach her without leaving the life I choose. Are there many who would love to meet a hundred-something gentleman, no matter how courteous he might be? Having guessed not, I have defined my new life.

A book to write. A puppy to walk and care for (even though he kidnaps my sneakers for a difficult time when I don't lock them away). And beautiful Puff, always ready to fly and land again on lakes and a calm sea. Intimate talks with the three?

Maybe so. I have much to learn.

$\mathcal{A}$ Strange and Mystical Event

IT HAPPENS OFTEN, they say. We're in the midst of our life, we take some photographs, think nothing unusual has happened. Then when we look at the pictures there's a spirit or an orb in the midst of our day! It's become a common event these days, with so many cameras at work. Strange, but common.

I didn't think that I'd have the experience. I was working on Puff, the little seaplane, doing some maintenance. For a friend, I laid out some parts on the deck, then got the camera and took several pictures.

To my surprise, well, to my astonishment!, there was an image that I had not seen when I pressed the shutter:

217

C hange of an Era

I T USED TO BE, that one could tell that a new era was happening. In electronics, it's happened, In publishing, it's happening, but the one I know best is aviation.

I remember the old pilots never much wanted to fly on instruments, reading headings and altitudes from the heading indicator and the altimeter, while all the world outside the windshield was grey fog. They called instrument flying "Needle-ball and alcohol," for the turn needle, the ball to show an airplane slipping or skidding, and the magnetic compass, damped with alcohol.

You could go anywhere you wanted with those crude

instruments. An airspeed indicator was nice to have, too. And an oil pressure gage for the engine.

Early pilots flew by the picture they saw, looking at the world outside of their open cockpits. They didn't enjoy "flying blind," but in the 1930's it was the beginning of an era, pretty well necessary if you wanted to fly every day.

Antoine de Saint-Exupery lived the first part of that new era. He didn't like modern planes, didn't much care for the P-38H (F-5) photo plane he flew at the end of the second world war.

He had lost many old friends, flying in the 20's and 30's, and the new era was not for him. He disappeared after what he had promised would be his last flight in the '38, July 31, 1944. Some said that he didn't really want to live while aviation changed and his friends had gone.

The next 50 or sixty years were the instrument era of aviation. Then all at once the era changed again, to digital instruments, and flat plate moving maps. All pretty colors to show one's position, altitude, restricted areas, terrain, weather, other airplanes in the sky.

Airplanes changed from steel and aluminum to carbon composite plastic forms, very slick and fast. And a strange thing. I don't much care for the new airplanes, the new era.

A few years ago, I down-shifted into very light aircraft, my little seaplane Puff has no flat-plate flying instruments, no digital engine instruments. She can fly perfectly well if I took every instrument out of the panel and left it on the ground. She's a simple day-flying airplane, fabric covering for her for wings and tail, she lands on a little strip of land, or when you wish, she lands of the surface of a lake of a calm sea.

This time in my life, I rarely stop at an airport. I care about quiet hidden places, I land by summer islands, most of them uninhabited. A little engine for Puff, a sliding transparent panel . . . you can open the cockpit with your elbow; an old-fashioned tail-wheel, simple retractable wheels, room for two people at most, and she's happiest with one.

It happened, then, I realized flying, that I felt just the same as Antoine de Saint-Exupery had felt. Aviation had passed me and my time. I had flown a fair amount of instrument hours when I had to be at big airports on time. But now? That's not me.

I am uninterested in modern aircraft, modern moving maps, electric motors to turn propellers. The sky that I have loved since I was six, has it changed, too?

If it has, there are a lot of us still caught in what is for us the golden age of flying. Maybe, a hundred years from now, everything of our time will be gone. But I hope there will stay that day some words we wrote, words from the past, telling of the sky we knew in an old era, and loved.

The Silent Ocean

AFTER A WHILE, one becomes lonely.

The "while," our researchers say, may be early for some, but after 70 or 80 years or so, it's common. Their studies tell us we can assume that long-term loneliness is an ancient belief in the bell-jars of mortal life, that our friends will be off for adventures away, leaving us to think we're alone on Earth.

If one of our friends was a wife or a husband, then our touch and our, "Good morning, dear one," will be lost over a wide calm ocean of silence.

I didn't think of this till a year or so ago. I learned there were not two, but three ways to die.

Sudden events: car crashes, lightning;

Slow events: illnesses, smoking;

And the third event: loneliness.

We barely realize it's happening, the third.

Sometimes former mates become wonderful friends.
Sometimes they learn how to change from mates to friends,
to live without romance, and without the angers that touch
many in the midst of separating.

Yet what happens is that the two don't play with words
they way they did before, no more the table-tennis with
ideas when each could say anything to the other. There's no
intimate sharing of thoughts, they don't have time or interest,
to tell each other what living feels like, the way once they did.

Romance is a color of life that they agree not to share. They'll
talk about most things, business and daily events, when they
might meet, but nothing that touches deeply, as though their
hearts were sealed from the story of our own personal joys
and fears.

Since I've chosen to live a life of distance from others (except
for writing, like now), loneliness tapped on my door for a long
time before I noticed.

Researchers say that men will lose some seven years of a
life alone, against the alternate life they'd share with their
partners. Living alone, one needs to search for one's purpose,

instead of knowing it in a mate's touch, or smile. Without her or him, there's no one to respond to words that once found bright echoes, once mattered to a close Other. We know we're separate, and we know there's a good chance we'll be separate for the rest of our lives.

The Internet, does that help? For some, they say. Internet relationships work well for those of the golden mean. If you're live at either end of the gold, you'll be untouched, and silent.

How can you tell someone you've just met, of the lifetimes you've lived till this minute, and learn about theirs? It will take a million words to say hello, unless they have a soulmate's touch of who you are, and you find the same within yourself.

If you had an old wind-up clock that ticked away the minutes, you can finally let it stop. Trouble is, when it stops ticking, it adds to the silence.

*E*veryone Can't, Anyone Can

I REMEMBER WHAT they used to tell us when we were children. They said, "You can't do that! What if everyone did that?"

Other moms told my friends that, and they told me, too. "What if everyone tried to do this?"

My mom never did. She said I could do anything I wanted to do, no matter what others did.

Was mom right, or were the other ones telling the truth? I'd think about that at night. If everyone wanted to be an actor, I thought, snuggled under the covers, what would the world be like?

There would be in all the Yellow Pages, just one letter: "A," for actors. No restaurants, no building contractors, no groceries, no pet shops, no psychiatrists. Just thousands of pages for Actors. Where did actors get automobiles? Where did they live? Where did 20th Century Fox find movie cameras, directors, guards at the gate, or even gates? Studios? Theaters? Offices? Film? Money? How would they do it, if everyone's an actor?

By the time the sun came up, it was clear to me that mom was right. There was zero chance that everyone would do whatever I wanted to do. Because the world, I had decided, would collapse.

So I tried my test. For my first job, I worked as a golf-ball picker at a driving range. Sure enough. I was alone there, golf balls whizzing left and right. Not one other person, not one, had decided to follow me. What a relief!

I tried what seemed like everything, after that. Delivering phone books, being a marine draftsman at a boat-building company, carrying the mail, flying for the Air Force, writing flight handbooks for Douglas Aircraft, writing for a magazine. Sure enough, I could do anything I wanted. The one little problem I found was that I couldn't hold a job longer than eight months.

The Air Force lasted a few years, because they'd shoot you if you left early.

So in civilian life, what to do? It was not just a little discomfort, after eight months, it was like a monster tearing out the bars of his cage . . . I'd do anything to quit!

Gradually I tried writing, the times I was out of work. I had a teacher in high school. John Gartner. He was the football coach, he ran the Creative Writing class, and he was a writer! He sold articles to magazines, he had published a series of books about a coach and the kids he taught.

And Mister Gartner changed my life, though I didn't know that for years.

The first day of that class, he said, "I know why you're here. This is not English Literature. It's an easy class." We shrank a bit in our seats. How did he know that?

"That's fine. I just want you to know, though, that the only way you'll get an A in this class, is when you show me the check you've earned for writing a story." We couldn't believe what we were hearing. "Simple," he said. "You don't have anything else to do in this class. You want your A, show me the check."

The man was cruel. I wanted to get A's from that easy class, and I couldn't do it!

He brought articles he had written, showed us chapter by chapter of his latest book, asked us what we thought of each one. "Incidents!" he told us, "Examples!"

Oh, I thought, there's a system that writers use! He showed us a check that came to him, held it between his two hands. "Your ideas," he said, "turn into money."

In the semester I wrote a story of an amateur astronomer group, grownups and a few kids, the telescopes they built, the sights they saw through eyepieces that looked like spaceship windows. Craters on the moon, the storms of Jupiter, double stars a gazillion miles away, the stories the adults told of what they had seen.

My story sold to the city's Sunday supplement. They sent me $26, less $4 for the photographs to illustrate it.

Came Monday, I brought that check to Mister Gartner. He nodded. "You've got your A, Richard."

Years later, that terrible boredom of jobs, finally listened to what John had done. I had written for money, when I was in high school!

I began writing when I was out of work. Writing was a little raft in the sea of unemployment. It sank. But the more I wrote, every time I left a job, the raft would sink a little more slowly. Finally, I wrote a book. and after that, after I left a job of flight instructing, I could just barely survive.

More stories, more books. Characters become friends, though they never lived in mortal bodies. Friends become spirit guides. Easy lessons, sometimes. Once in a while a difficult test. Yet each one was a blessing as soon as I learned I had asked for its lesson, deep in the subconscious, and sure enough, it appeared. Just recently I began calling them blessings, even when they seemed to be difficult tests. Sooner or later I would call them lessons, I thought, why not call them blessings at once, instead of being forced to acknowledge them at the end?

After a while, in one of my later blessings, I learned that there's no such thing as death. It's walking from a mortal room to a spiritual one, no pain, light and color, our consciousness leaving in a coma while the body decides to survive, or not.

I've discovered, I think, that every story we live, every test we pass, is important to our lives.

Some are funny (why did I insist on sleeping under the wing of my airplane when an old-time barnstormer with me stayed in the best hotel in town?), some are remarkable (before I went out to fly, a friend sent me a spare propeller I never wanted, a week before I hit a hidden back-furrow with my propeller, bent it at high speed), some are startling (why did I hear a voice "*Jonathan Livingston Seagull*," before I knew what the story was about?).

Everyone can't have a life like ours. But we can. Gradually I'm getting the idea that learning never stops, during our life on Earth. I think that maybe we can take a vacation while we're in the afterlife. Can we fly an airplane that won't crash? What a great idea!

*I*t's Hard To Tell By Looking

*I'*LL BET that the man in the front cockpit of that T-28 doesn't look much different to you from any other instructor pilot you've known.

It's hard to tell by looking, but Jamie V. Forbes was one of those few men whose sheer quiet character taught me more than the hundred-some hours we flew together.

"This isn't in the syllabus, but you probably ought to know how to do a snap-roll off the top of a loop," he said. And, "Settle down, Mister Bach. The airplane flies itself. All you have to do is guide it."

Words I still hear him speak, and it's been 55 years since. Jamie Forbes was hired to teach us how to control an airplane; what he taught was how to control ourselves. He did that without a word on the subject, he showed us by being the man he was. Never once did he raise his voice, even when we screwed up something awful, spinning out of the top of our loop instead of snap-rolling, drifting below approach minimums, distracted setting some radio frequency.

"You might want to notice your altitude about now, Mister Bach, unless you intend for us to purchase some agricultural real estate . . ."

He didn't say look out for this, look out for that. "You can do anything you want to in an airplane," always that hint of a smile, "until you hit the ground."

Not, "Stay calm when you're flying, no matter what." He showed us, his even voice through the midst of what sometimes seemed to us like hell breaking loose. He let us find the words. My translation, "If I've got to be scared in an airplane, I'll be scared after I land. Right now I fly the machine." Mister Forbes figured our take would last longer than his, that his job was to be these kids' example of what a pilot ought to be.

He died many years ago, but if somehow we met today, Mr. Forbes, would neither recognize me nor remember we had flown together. Best I can tell, he had thousands of students. Yet who he was soaked so deeply into who I am that when time came to name the hero of *Hypnotizing Maria,* to show the heart of the truest pilot I could imagine, I named him Jamie Forbes.

You and I remember the best instructors in our lives. What we may not remember, chances are, is that we've been the same for someone else, and never knew it.

S ine qua non:
   "Without which, Nothing."

I T NEVER would have happened, this scene, under zero conditions would ever I have stood on this beach, heard this cool water whispering in the sand, felt that breeze across the water, were it not for the machine you see here, colored maroonish-white.

Is that what they had in mind, the ones who labored and failed, labored and won the inventions of flight? "It's not the machine that matters," would they have said, "it's the experience that the machine will bring to lives unborn!"

No way they would have said that, my guess. More likely it was the machine that mattered to Wilbur and Orville, to Taylor and his Cub, though perhaps not to Mr. Piper, when he bought the Cub from Taylor and Jamaneau, named it after himself and made it famous around the world.

Inventors love building amazing things, bolt by bolt; visionaries love building ideas, to which things are servant.

So whom do I thank, standing on this shore, drawing this day into my now and memories-to-be? Inventors, thank you. Visionaries, thank you. Yet of course that beach would not exist without my own decision to make it come true. So thank me, too?

What made me choose flying in the first place? Fantasies of heaven, of soaring above clouds, of reliving days of soul without body? Getting close.

Love, it comes down to. Irresistible attraction to some invisible that matters more than matter does, the spirit behind the molecules.

Key to happiness, I've ever thought: Find what we most love in all the world, and go that way.

The hard thing is not the struggle of going-that-way, no matter the jungles and thorns that lie in that direction. The hard thing, the doorway to a lifetime of mediocrity, is *not finding what it is that we love.*
The History of Toy Soldiers, or Can I Build A House from Toothpicks? or I Love Advertising! ... doesn't matter what it is we love, the object is immaterial.

Live without some love, though, we're doomed.

So what's the ultimate *sine qua non?*

You guessed it.

*T*he Almost-Secret Diary

*H*OW CAN I do this? How can I say some things, share some ideas that are really not for everyone to see?

Do I want *everyone* to know the odd and sometimes the dear ideas of my book? Do I gather ideas that have meant so much to me, do I set them loose for the public where drivers on the way to Other Places run them down, barely noticing?

My little ideas are . . . well, they're the sheep I once mentioned in *Illusions II*. Some of them, some day, may be written in stories, some just want to be set free without a book to sail them around the world.

They are valuable sheep, here on this little meadow, a

magical land for them to live and gently to meet us.

Here's a few words about the sheep from the book:

****

Shimoda took a little book from his shirt pocket, opened it. He looked at me, not at the page, and told me what the words said: *"Nobody comes to Earth to dodge problems. We come here to take 'em on."*

I hope not me, I thought. I'll dodge this problem, please. "I have to take my memories for true. Not an image, this is my memory! I was one inch from . . ." I blinked. "Your *Messiah's Handbook!* It's still with you?

"You've promised to believe what you remember, even when it isn't true? This is not the Handbook. It's . . ." he closed the book, read the title: ". . . *Lesser Maxims and Short Silences.*"

"Lesser Maxims? Not as powerful as the *Handbook*?"

He handed the little book to me,

Why you and why now? Because you asked it to be this way.

This disaster is the chance you prayed for, your wish come true.

I prayed for this? Nearly dying? I don't remember praying for an airplane crash. Why was this event the one I prayed for? Why me?

Because it was right on the edge of impossible, that's why.

Because it would require absolute determination, day after week, month after month, and then it could have a host of difficulties. I needed to know whether my beliefs would overcome every one of the problems.

The doctors were required to talk about what could happen, how my life would never be the same again. I'd be required to smother every one of their beliefs with my own, with beliefs I called true. They could call on all of the knowledge of material Western medicine, I could call on spirit, hold to it even though no one could see it. *I am a perfect expression of perfect Love, here and now.*

That mattered to me more than living in this world. I didn't know that, before.

I shook my head, turned Shimoda's page.

* * * *

Unsuccessful Animal Inventions:

Wolves on Stilts.

* * * *

"Wolves on Stilts? How does that affect my life, Don?"

"It's a Lesser Maxim. It may not affect your life at all."

"Oh. Who wrote this odd book? You keep it in your pocket."

"You."

"M."

"You don't believe me, do you?"

"N."

"Turn to the last page."

I did. I had written an introduction, my caring for the sheep of ideas never printed, signed my name to it.

"*Wolves on stilts?*"

"You're kind," he said. "How many sheep would love to see the wolves practicing?"

I smiled. "Some. Never published? I forget."

****

True. Never published. For now, I want to put them on this website. Yet now they're private thoughts, an almost-secret diary, thoughts that touched me but not ready to publish, they may never be.

Here's the introduction for the several hundred of my little sheep.

NOT EVERYONE who's an idea makes it into a book.

Pour all our bright sparks into writing a novel, half of them get cut, vanished in rewrite to the Power of the Deleted Word.

Cutting the unnecessary makes for a wonderful story, sure

enough: it's a crisp free arrow; last sentence ties all before in some happy shock-wave for a reader, stays in mind, maybe, for hours.

I love books like that: love to read 'em, do my best to paint them to words, too.

Writers get well into their career, though, and here's all these lost sheep, knee-high, following us about, all the ideas that never made it to a page of those lean stories. They don't complain, they're not sad. But a writer is their shepherd, and those fluffy unpublished maxims, they don't stray.

Ever.

Couple or five decades, writing, you've got a fair flock about you, meandering when you walk, galloping alongside while you run. Shepherd you are, but not their keeper. Their true keepers are readers out there in the world who want them for pets, put them to work solving problems, breaking deadlocks, lifting sorrows with a smile, every day, daily life.

I don't know what other writers do with their flocks. I didn't know what to do with mine till I found them yet again, grazing in my *Edit This Out* file, my *Deleteds from Final Draft*—maxims who delighted me when we met, who had helped me remember, kept me warm through my shares of ice and winter.

So came the day, I feel this tug on my pant-leg, I look down and it's a spokes-sheep:

"You love us?" she said, big dark eyes, earnest, asking. "We've helped you, and you love us still?"

I knelt down, drew it close.

"Of course I love you! I owe my songs to you, my visions of who we are!"

"Your readers, Richard," she said. "Don't they have songs too, and visions?"

"Of course, silly sheep! Readers are same as me . . . all of us have our musics."

"Then we want to be with them. We want to be . . ." the little creature looked to the ground, then back to me, " . . we want to be useful."

Whoa, I thought. I didn't say anything.

"We're not for everyone, of course. We'll be chased off some hillsides: *Out! Bad idea! Not welcome! Shoo!*"

I nodded. Smart sheep: nobody's welcome everywhere.

"We know we don't belong in the books you've written, but that doesn't mean we're not true for some readers, now and then. Doesn't mean we shouldn't have a chance."

Having said what she had to say, the little thing trusted her way back toward the others. She wanted me to know. She had told me. Her job was done. I would do whatever I would do for the future of her flock.

****

You know what I decided, of course, for here they are.

246

Now they're your flock, too, in your hands. Some may come with a laugh, some won't matter, some might save your life . . . they've saved mine a couple times over.

****

To a new writer:

What you're doing now is pouring a block of molten words.

You'll be shaping it, when it cools, with a sledge and chisels, with sandpaper and last of all, with one soft cloth.

****

Call me overcautious, but that's the last time I go surfing without my parachute.

****

Why does it take the four-year-old so long, to learn to read?

1. Download the Cyrillic alphabet.

2. Start your timer.

3. When you're reading Russian as well as your child's reading English, stop the clock.

****

They go on. For folks like me, these little sheep are friends. I don't know how to use them right now, but I can't erase them, either.

Yet, one can't have too many sheep.

And one never wants to delete them.

Note: *What you are about to read is pure fiction. Any similarity between the characters in the following story and anyone else, living or dead, is pure coincidence. The story is a fable, with a moral, strictly for those readers who enjoy fictitious fables with morals. It is not a true story.*

A Story in Fiction

ONCE THERE WAS a husband and wife, Roger and Susan. Roger wrote books about their adventures, part fiction but a lot of non-fiction, too.

Then one day Roger and Susan discovered that each wanted a different future. He wanted to continue to drive to all the small towns in the country and to write about them, she to rest from the constantly increasing workload of managing his books in many editions and languages around the world.

She had a right to choose a quiet future, he had a right to choose an active one, and neither wished to force the other to live as they did not want to live.

After careful thought, after many discussions, and for reasons that at last made perfect sense to each of them, the two separated and divorced, wishing love and happiness to the other.

Susan made one request, however: she asked Roger please never to mention her name on his books or his website. Unless she chose to write about herself, she said, and unless readers chose to buy her books, what she did in her private life was nobody's business but her own.

Roger agreed. He knew that a reader's right to know a writer's personal choices stops at the last page of any writer's book.

He promised not to mention her name, and the two went their different ways, each grateful to the other for powerful lessons learned from their long marriage.

Most readers know that the end of a marriage is an enormously complex event, and his readers trusted that Roger and Susan probably had not taken the step to divorce one afternoon on a lark, for the fun of it, because they had nothing else to do.

A tiny fraction of visitors to his website, though, did not accept the news, nor did they recognize that Susan had a right to live her own quiet life.

These few badgered poor Roger: "Where's Susan? How dare you separate? We trusted you when you said that you loved each other, and by divorcing you have shattered our world! Your books, once truth, are now lies! We shall never believe in love again—we despise you both, and everything you stand for!"

While he realized that his readers were free to be distressed,

Roger also realized his mistake. He had forgotten to remind that last one percent of his readers that each is an independent person, responsible for her or his own independent choices.

He had forgotten, in the book about his life with Susan, to insert one last sentence:

Everything in this book may be wrong.

*O*n Tour

SOMETIMES, and often on a book tour, someone asks, "What are you working on now?"

"Nothing," is my answer, "and I hope never to write another book so long as I might live."

I like answers that start simple and go from there. I like this one because it suggests a truth, at least a truth for me: before one starts writing a book one hasn't the faintest idea what one is getting into.

By the time one has written a few books, time mercifully erases the fact that one's life is taken over from the moment one agrees to loan one's heart and hands to a lovely idea.

All that loss-of-control disappears in the glare of an idea's singular beauty, in the delight that one will be able to get close to something, unwritten, so desperately lovely.

"Never again" reminds me: forget about the rest of your life, Richard, forget it in the moment you let that light embrace you. All else goes pale in the dance with words and it's not easy to break out, to focus one's attention on paying the electric bill though it be nearly due.

Practically speaking, "Never again" reminds us, reader and writer, that either of us may decide at any minute to ascend beyond our current consent to the appearances of our little planet, and the book just published could well be the last ever to find its way to print.

"Never again" warns not to do what once I did, years ago.

I was caught by a charming story idea, had begun writing, and happily shared the theme with a stranger who asked kindly what I might be writing. I said not only what had been written, but told him where I thought the story was going to go, and it was all of it wonderful fun.

Next day, when I sat down to write, the story had gone flat and dull. When I touched the keyboard, no matter what words I chose, an echo in my mind, "You've said this before. This is old news." No longer spontaneous, the story had lost its surprise and delight for me, they had been removed from the process of writing. I don't remember whether I finished it or not.

That was the last time I told anyone what I was writing before the manuscript was finished. When the writing is done, however, I'm a veritable chatterbox about the story, though I never tell it as well as it was written, and now I'm practicing shutting up about a book even after it's published.

If they really want to know what I've been writing, the answer is waiting in the bookstore.

*N*evil Shute, the Day He Died

*O*NE OF MY FAVORITE writers in all the world was Nevil Shute. I was given a copy of his last manuscript, *Incident at Eucla*, on which he was working when he died.

The author of *On the Beach, The Rainbow and the Rose, Round the Bend, Trustee from the Toolroom* and twenty-some other strikingly original and beautiful books, Shute began this last novel with his typical skilled sunrise: calm, slow, even, rational. Yet behind the care, we can sense the power of an idea, building.

As the narrator drives toward Eucla, on the southern coast of Australia, we know something immense is about to happen and we are certain that we are going to be standing at ground zero when it does.

The book is delight, driven by the skill of a man who was the most popular living English author of his time, toward an event we can almost begin to grasp.

His last sentence: "There was a fluffy haired young girl with them, helping somewhat ineffectually and she was weeping, the tears running quietly down her cheeks."

Then the manuscript stops. Stops! Cold. No more words. Blank paper. That day, Nevil Shute died.

The feeling, curled up with the manuscript forty years later, is that of hurtling along in a Rolls-Royce limousine, at very high speed, and in the blink of an eye we find that our driver has disappeared and the Rolls has gone mid-air off the edge of a cliff.

It was that shocking, for me, I felt that helpless. I cried, for the loss of a man I never met.

Should ever we wonder if one individual can be important, then reading that half-manuscript will help us understand.

Important? No. Too tame. Essential for the existence of the world as we know it, without whom we shall live in a different universe.

No one will know what was waiting to happen at Eucla. Every word that Nevil Shute would have used to finish that book is with us this moment. Yet no one alive can imagine just which ones he would have used, to write his next simple sentence.

It's easy to echo what a writer has already written. Try predicting what next she or he is going write. Do that, and we will watch ourselves define the term, "pale imitation."

Each of us, no matter our calling: absolutely, totally, unpredictably, irreplaceably, one-of-a-kind unique.

The Football and Mister Wood

*I*N JUNIOR HIGH SCHOOL, you were a Soshe or you were a Square. No one defined one from the other.

Later I guessed that Soche was short for "Social" and Square was short for you weren't.

The Soches were the cool guys, the Dangerous-Rebel guys and the way-pretty Alpha girls. If you've seen The Fonz from the old television show—he was a Soche.

The two groups had little to do with each other by choice, but we were forced to share classes with each other, as that was what school was for, after all: training in our common culture.

One class we shared, unfortunately, was Physical Education, and one day a year we were required to take a test with a football, to see how far each of us could throw it and kick it and how fast we could run with it down a stretch of track.

I had not exactly welcomed the day of the test, as I had just discovered the stories of a writer named Ray Bradbury and much preferred tramping Mars with him than the track with the like of Ricky Conn, the school's Marlon Brandoesque Super-Soche, cocky, confident, and Look Out For Me.

Well described, for clearly he spent more time working out with weights than I spent in the school library. Girls who loved hard bodies and risk, they loved Ricky Conn.

Came the day of the test, I don't know why but our regular Phys Ed teacher was absent. In his place appeared Mister Wood, the bespectacled teacher of Metal Shop, and as I recall, Vice-Principal of the school, as well. Most everyone liked Mister Wood, and perhaps that's why Ricky didn't.

While Mister Wood explained what the rules were for our football test, how many tries we got at each division, Ricky was chattering away to anyone who'd listen. Mister Wood looked at him once, as I recall, a knock-off-the-chatter-please look, which apparently Ricky took for a challenge.

After the teacher said, "Do your best, guys, to throw the ball as hard and as far as you can," came Ricky's voice, "Yeah, Teach, I can throw the ball so hard nobody can catch it!" Big confident grin.

Mister Wood took his time, turned and faced Ricky directly. "That's not true, Conn," he said. "I can catch any ball you can throw."

It had been fairly quiet on the field, except for Ricky's comments, but just then it got awfully quiet indeed.

With everybody else standing there, I watched Ricky as though he were a sudden statue on his pedestal. He wasn't a statue. For a second he froze startled, and then a slow smile spread, as if he couldn't believe his luck.

The metal-shop teacher, the Vice-Principal—you heard it— was asking for a showdown with the Rickster!

Mister Wood tossed the football to Ricky. They stood for a moment perhaps twelve feet apart, us slowly backing out of the way, as though the field was a Dodge City saloon and something violent was about to happen. It wasn't Dodge City, but it was violent.

Ricky's smile faded, he lofted the ball a couple of times, gently, getting the feel of it. He bent down a bit, then whipped upright, shot his arm like lightning and fired a bullet-pass as hard as he could, straight at Mister Wood's chest.

That moment is frozen in my mind, which had set its shutter-speed at a thousandth of a second. Mister Wood's glasses went flying forward as the ball hit his chest, snapping his head back.

The ball would have bounced twenty feet from his body had not Mister Wood caught it with one hand, and with its last force left, the ball made a single little hop in the air, and came to rest in the crook of Mister Wood's arm.

One of the boys stepped over and picked up his glasses from

the ground, handed them back. "Thank you," said Mister Wood.

About there my mind ran out of film. I don't recall whether anyone applauded, I don't remember what happened then except we took our test and counted our best of three tries at kicking the thing and so forth.

Today, Mister Wood is long dead. He was gray-haired before that day, and that day was . . . let me count . . . sixty-two years ago. I didn't tell him wow; didn't know I'd never forget, but I haven't. I didn't learn till a few years ago that before he was a metal shop teacher, he had been a quarterback on a professional football team

That day Mister Wood showed Ricky Conn and he showed the rest of us what sheer calm courage looks like, close-up.

Wordless teaching, by way of conflict resolution, boys, here's a bit of what I think being a man might be.

Oh, that's physical education! Thank you, Mister Wood!

*I*s Suicide a Sin?

I DON'T KNOW HOW I got on the subject, but I found myself looking up "suicide sin" on the Internet. Do other people think it is?

There were quite a few arguments by folks who care about sin, declaring that God doesn't want us to kill ourselves except, I'm guessing, if we let the infidels do it for us in a holy war.

Then it occurred to me, that Jesus the Christ is the first major celebrity suicide that comes swiftly to mind, after Socrates. If Jesus killed himself, why is it a sin for me to do the same? Is Jesus a sinner?

It was not so long ago that the moralities about suicide made sense to me. Talking with a friend, just retired as a police officer, he shared a few stories from his career, his experience with what the police department calls, "Suicide by Cop."

Some cornered murderer or bank robber is holed up in a house, tracked down and surrounded by police. "Come out of the house with your hands up!"

In time he does, hands up, but he's holding a gun.

"Keep your hands up, drop the gun, turn around and face the wall!"

No response.

"Drop the gun, please, now!"

Instead, and occasionally with a smile, my friend told me, the man will extend the hand which holds the gun, and point it toward the police. Whereupon, of course, he collapses in a hail of gunfire.

Later it's found, sometimes, that his gun was not loaded. The man chose to die, but he asked the police to do the suiciding for him.

How is this different from the story of Jesus' death, except that Jesus had perhaps a thousand different opportunities to escape and the criminal may have had three or four?

Jesus chose to die, and asked the authorities to do it for him: "Suicide by Roman."

I'm not the only one who's wondered about this. There's a line by the Judas character in *Jesus Christ Superstar*. Before he runs to "betray" Jesus, he asks him, "What if I just stayed here and ruined your ambition?"

Most of Western civilization is so familiar with the story that we think it was essential for Jesus to kill himself. Not so, of course, as soon as we ask, "Essential for what?"

Essential for the story to turn out as we know it. Had the story changed, had he decided to repair to France with Mary Magdalen, Jesus would have led a different life, teaching and writing and playing with his children. And the world would not have had to endure the blessing and the curse of Christianity for the last 2100 years.

Kill himself he did, though, so the story goes. It was certainly his freedom to do so; I just wonder why so many of his followers consider their leader's own example to be sinful.

Perhaps after they think of his choices, and in the light of his story, they will change their minds and declare it isn't sinful at all.

$\mathcal{M}$y Rorschach World

$\mathcal{S}$OMETIMES ON A DOG WALK, I wonder what's happened to my dogs. We walk in a wilderness place that they know well, so they take off for a while and I'm all alone on the path.

When I stand outside myself, or float a few hundred feet in the air, I look down at me and ask, "What's that guy doing, the only soul in sight?" And then I smile at the answer, "He's walking his dogs."

Yesterday, after they abandoned me, I had a chance to notice the last of the snow on the ground, scattered patterns here and there. This patch looked like a lion, that like a spaceship, the last one like an angel.

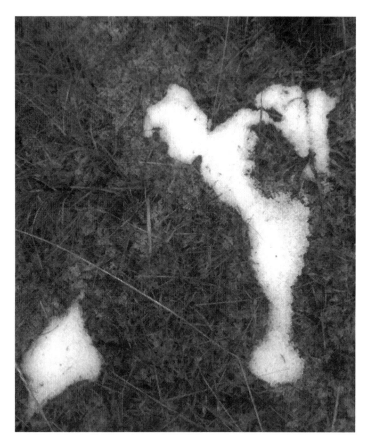

I laughed when I noticed that I was using the snow for my personal Rorschach test.

Then I wondered; instead of ink-blots or snow-blots, what if I use the world around me for my test? This stack of massive logs, I saw it first as a barrier, an obstacle, "Don't Go Here!" Then it shifted itself to be a ladder, easy to climb for a clearer view of my landscape.

The path itself, does it represent my own path, I wondered, hard going up hillsides sometimes, curving later around peaceful glades? Why of course it does ... that path is my life!

I'd been walking the same physical road for years, unaware that it stands for my destiny, whenever I choose to see it that way. Rocks, trees, sky, city, cars, people—the physical expressions, they're pictures of my mental and spiritual surroundings, as well.

By the time the pups came dashing back to join me, I saw them as travelers with me along our way, not talking but setting an example: what's wrong with running your path sometimes instead of walking, what's wrong with letting the destination take care of itself and simply being, for a while?

Pretend every so-called external thing stands for something internal, and what all of a sudden do we understand about ourselves and about our spiritual choice to visit this planet?

If the pups could talk, I'd ask them. Yet if they could talk, they'd probably say nothing, just let me figure it out for myself.

*T*ruthful Arguments

*H*ER HUSBAND WAS UPSET. "I can't believe you forgot our anniversary! And you never remember, last year it was the same thing! I've got to admit, you're just plain thoughtless, you know how important this day is to me, and you don't care one bit how I feel . . . I'd swear you go out of your way to hurt me!"

Melanie listened. When he paused, frustrated, she said, "Jack, I love you. Your truthful argument, please?"

His face still dark with anger, her husband all at once relaxed, and laughed. "Do you insist?"

She smiled. "I insist, sweetheart."

"Very well," he said. "My Truthful Argument." He leaned against the kitchen counter. "Among the many choices available to me, I chose to be upset, just now. I made that choice because in that moment it seemed to me, and I may be wrong, that you haven't remembered today is our anniversary.

"However: my greater truth is that you've remembered more times than you've forgotten.

"However: you are so consistently kind and thoughtful of me in so many other ways, just now I realize that calendars don't matter.

"My truth, my perception from the huge majority of my impressions and memories, is that you care for me so much you decided to spend your life with me, no matter I sometimes lose my perspective and my temper, too, from time to time, when I think I've lost your love.

"My truth is I know that not you, not anyone has the power to hurt me or upset me or to anger me but myself, and to the best of my knowledge you have no more tried to hurt me in ten years being married than I've tried to hurt you. And that is never.

"You are no more thoughtless than I am. You're a galaxy of thoughts! Both of us, we sometimes think in different directions and that's OK, isn't it? It makes for a rich wide star-field for us to explore together."

He smiled. "And by the way," he said, "Happy Anniversary."

She moved close, touched his shoulder. "Thank you for

telling me your truth," she said. "If you're hungry, we should probably go to the bedroom. There's ten candles in there, burning down."

The reason I love that little story is the However parts. For every insult we'd like to hurl when we're angry, there's a raft of howevers: "You're so mean to me! However, truth be told, you are many more times kind than mean."

"You're so different from me! However, to tell the truth, we have a lot more sames than differents."

"I hate you! However, we've shared many more warm kind times than hateful and in truth I love you more than anyone in the world."

Try it, next argument. Begin to respond in anger, then add the word, "however, . . . " and tell the truth you know despite your distress.

See how rage disappears in laughter?

*I*f You Build It, It Will Fly

YOU CAN HAVE the world's best toolkit, but when there's no patience there, you're probably not going to build anything that makes you much happier.

For this reason, and although I wanted to build an airplane, I knew it wouldn't happen. Wouldn't, that is, until the ultra-light flying machines came on the market.

They seemed so simple! Simple aluminum tubes, simple steel cables, you pop some fabric on the wings, wheels on axles, engine on mount, you're done!

That's pretty well the way it worked out. I don't remember how many hours it took to assemble my Pterodactyl

Ascender, but it didn't feel like a whole lot.

One day it lay in brown cardboard boxes, long coffins on the garage floor, the next day the boxes were gone and there was a great deal of unrecognizable odd parts on the floor.

Next day it was all still there, me at the kitchen table reading the manual of how it was all supposed to fit together. Before I knew it, I had finished reading the first chapter of the manual.

The parts were still on the floor. They stayed there as I began Section Two, "Assembling the Wing."

A month later, perhaps two months, I was all suited up for the first flight, engine started, checklist complete: Wings—Installed. Wheels—On. Engine—Running. No brakes but heels dug into ground. Ready?

Since I had built this thing, or at least assembled it, I wasn't expecting it to fly.

I have assembled a fair number of things: a child's bicycle, two outdoor tables, a lawnmower, bookshelves aplenty. None of them flew, so how could this thing of cloth and frail metals do what they could not?

Yet I pretended that what I had assembled was actually an airplane, if a small one, and deserved my best effort. Such as: Throttle Forward—Lift Feet.

The frail thing was so light . . . one blast from the engine and it took off, egg from a slingshot. In less than a hundred-feet it was in the air, forest of treetops suddenly below, climbing like an ancient dragon, flying, and bearing me with it!

The cockpit was a little sparse. I reached for my pencil to make a note on my kneeboard, dropped the pencil and watched it disappear, a thousand feet down.

At two thousand feet I shut the engine down, as the advertisement had said it might be a reasonably good glider. It was.

Silent save for the soft breeze, we circled in rising air. Perhaps we didn't gain much altitude, but for sure we weren't following the pencil, not at all.

Pitch control so light and sensitive that much more than a touch reared the dragon skyward or plunged it down. Note to self: fly the pitch control as you would a helicopter's . . . just think about climbing and don't move your hand; that'll be plenty.

I reached up for the engine start handle, pulled the cord and I had a power-plane once more. A few turns and stalls, power on power off . . . what a sweet little machine!

Throttle back, a steep descent to the hayfield, level out inches above the grass and hold off . . . till the main wheels brush the ground, nosewheel comes down to follow, feet out when I dared, for brakes.

And there we were, engine perking quietly behind me, sounding exhilarated itself—"Want to try it again, boss?"

That sounded like a good idea.

$\mathcal{N}$ormally I Wouldn't Fly

$\mathcal{T}$HIS CLOSE TO a wilderness mountain ridge.

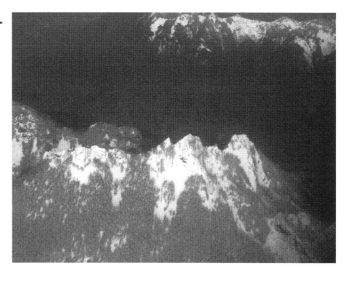

I can see the smile of my first flight instructor, all cool and unconcerned, pulling the throttle to idle and saying, "By the way, where do you plan to land when the engine quits . . . as it just has?"

"I guess we'll have to put 'er down on the little pointy white place," I'd say.

But really, between you and me, and if you tilt your page just right, you can see the valley beyond and a field down there that'd be not so hard to slip into and land, get out and stretch our legs, rest a bit from flying.

Like so many threats in our lives, a ferocious foreground distracts from our background security. It's fun to be scared, sometimes, but never to fear that our true life can be lost, nor in the slightest danger.

The Lasting Benefit of Early Starvings

I DISCOVERED THIS in the days when Kraft Dinner was fifteen cents for the box and there weren't many boxes in the pantry.

No, I am not here complaining, I am celebrating! Because one day back then, as I was surveying the last of the ice cream and it looked as if I wouldn't be seeing any such thing for the next decade, I thought, I wonder if I can extend this a bit, before they turn off the electricity.

It was in such a mood of scientific experimentation, willing to lose everything, that I moved as though in trance, set the ice cream container under the water faucet and ran a little hydrogen hydroxide directly over what was left in the container—chocolate, as I recall.

I was cautious, so allowed much less water than ice cream. For a few seconds after I did this, it looked as though someone had poured water on the ice cream. Which wasn't all that successful looking, so I reached down with a spoon and squashed it together, liquid and solid, stirred it, tentatively. Then I added just a bit more water, stirring, not shaking.

I'll bet you're thinking it looked like melted ice cream, but . . . Well, it did look like melted ice cream, but listen to this: It wasn't!

When ice cream melts it does one thing: it melts.

But when ice cream is thinned with water it does something else, it freezes the dihydrogen monoxide into tiny crystals which are then stirred into a non-melted result which I call, "Water in Ice Cream," or, "Water in Sherbet."

Waitresses, when I order this dish today, or ask for a milk shake made with water, do not believe about the crystals, but they bring me the result if I pay them to do it.

Even now, you're curious about this, aren't you? You don't believe me, or can't imagine that common hydroxic acid behaves in such a delicious way when stirred coldly into a dish of I.C. or India Charlie as we say in aviation.

Yes, it stretches the basic supply by some fifteen percent, but more, it tastes really cool.

You think I'm kidding, don't you?

The Kid

I REMEMBER HIM, I remember that kid in the fighter-bomber, photo taken Spring of 1962, Chaumont Air Base, France. It wasn't even my airplane, the one I spent weekends polishing.

It was the closest plane on the flight line that day, and I was the closest pilot, and the Information Officer said we need a photo for the base newspaper . . . "Lieutenant, would you mind hopping up into the cockpit and sort of pretending you're going to fly?"

I looked around, there was no other pilot on the line. "Sure. You want it with a hat, I guess, if I'm going to fly?"

"A hat?"

"A flying helmet . . . a crash helmet. We don't really fly unless we've got a hat . . . "

"Yes, please."

I went and got my hat, and hopped up into the cockpit and fastened the oxygen mask and pulled the visor down.

"Could you leave the rubber thing loose, and the glass up? We want to see . . . otherwise you're a . . . "

machine, I thought. Otherwise you're a faceless machine. I raised the visor, squinted a bit in the sunlight, unsnapped the oxygen mask.

"That's good. Could you don't look at the camera? Like you're about to take off."

"If I were about to take off, I'd close the canopy," I said. And I'd have the mask on and the visor down and I'd pull the safety pins out of the landing gear and if I really wanted to fly I'd probably start the engine."

"No, leave the hatch open. Maybe look over about there, please? Good. A little more to the left . . . "

In a minute he said thank you and he and the photographer walked away. When I got down from the airplane I didn't think I'd be back to visit me 50 years later and I'd be calling me Kid.

I flew some training mission that afternoon, then went home

to the barracks and typed a chapter that night that I didn't know would be published, under a title I hadn't thought of: *Stranger to the Ground.*

Forgot about the photo, didn't realize that hundredth of a second would caption my military career and the career of every other fighter pilot in history: *Force*.

Part of life in space-time, even now. We want to move something, we force it till it moves. From gentle to explosive, that's the way it's been all these centuries: push comes to shove.

Now I grant that blowing up things, especially for kids, is a whole lot of fun. Or at least it is until it's your friends blowing up, or you.

Connect your mask, lower your visor, close the canopy, run that throttle forward and you are a machine.

But once in a while the machine climbs down from the cockpit at the end of the mission, and it realizes that it may have killed somebody today. And that's a good thing that's what I'm here for and I'll get a colored ribbon for it and let's support our troops and why have I stopped sleeping at night?

Why do I have the same dream over and over, of that little house flying all slow-motion into the air, and the debris that was the family, I didn't really see them coming apart, too, did I?

Collateral damage if you want to make an omelet you're gonna break some eg

They weren't eggs. For a second they looked like little girls, and then they didn't.

Oh, you kid. You poor beloved innocent stupid kid, volunteered to be killer-for-pay.

Win them ribbons now.

You'll be talkin' to 'em later.

*B*oxers Train for Boxing, Soldiers Train for War

*I*T WAS A BIT OF A CHALLENGE, I remember, to watch poor Sylvester Stallone get himself pummeled nearly to death on screen in the first Rocky motion picture.

[INSERT PHOTO OF BLOODY WRECKED ROCKY BALBOA THAT I DON'T HAVE THE COURAGE TO POST ALTHOUGH THE PICTURE IS IMPORTANT TO MY STORY SO PLEASE IMAGINE IT HERE AND CONTINUE READING]

I got more used to it as the series continued, but even when I knew Rocky wasn't really getting killed, it was just a movie, the images got so gruesome that I stopped watching after two.

I couldn't help it. I felt so sorry! for him, every time he got up he's hit by another railroad train. I wished there were some-thing I could do, anything to end the pain and the blood and the wrecking of dear Rocky, so kind at heart.

All I needed was a few years to think about it, and that quick, the answer hit me like a big fluffy Spaulding glove: Rocky's no victim, Richard, he chose to be a boxer!

That blinked me, the implications of his choice. Why am I focusing my concern and my wish-to-rescue on the scenes where Rocky's getting crushed, while I don't mind the scenes where he's crushing somebody else?

After all, wasn't Rocky working those months and years, long and hard, practicing to hurt others in the most violent way he could, short of dragging a chain-saw into the ring which would be pretty hard to operate in boxing gloves anyway? Rocky knew he'd probably take a hit now and then, I'm sure he knew his opponents would be well-trained and powerful and bigger than . . . well, bigger than gerbils.

But even so, knowing that, he chose to be a boxer anyway!

From time to time I've met folks I'd like to rescue. That is, my way of living the world in the moment we met, seemed to me less stressful than their way of living it.

I forgot the moments of my own past, scenes when I was stranded in some wilderness with an airplane that could no longer fly or broke or bankrupt, my just-let-me-die-now days.

Somebody looking in would have said, "Poor broken thing! Won't anyone help, someone come fix his plane for him, give him money, help him out, at least find some food for him instead of all he's got is charcoal pan-bread and engine oil?"

Lucky me, no such bad luck as rescue from others. I wanted to be a flyer. I quit other jobs, deliberately quit them, to be a writer. Flyers crash, writers starve.

I knew that, going in. Rocky chose boxing. Soldiers choose battle. We train for our destinies, with every choice along the way.

Times come often, after a lot of training, all at once the chips slam down and we're beating somebody or getting beaten, we're killing somebody or we're getting killed, we've earned a fortune or we're in the street lost every dime.

Why? Best answer I could find, it's still with me today: We love show-biz.

Lead us to action-adventure with all the faux-risk that comes with beliefs of separation from undying Life, from perfect Love, and we dive right in, go for our close-up on-screen, prove our power to survive any punch space-time can throw, because we're more than space-time ever imagined we can be.

We're spirit, space-time! Punch that!

Soon as I came to know I'm the guy responsible, I'm the one got me into this mess, I figured that somewhere in my invisible tool kit there was likely a way to get out of it, to dismount from disaster by my own double-somersault to a stand-up landing.

When I'm in the middle of my somersaults, I'm not hoping for somebody to say poor-thing-he-can't-possibly-survive, for a well-meaning soul to net me mid-air and lower me safely to the mat. I've got my show to finish, and I'll finish it my way thank you!

Watch lives, read biography. Double-somersaults everywhere, triples brought off with blinding skill. Once in a while somebody crashes, sure enough, split-second wrong choice.

Yet the performance we most treasure is the one by the soul who crashed last time, she picked herself up and started over,

came back and finished with the flying open dismount to her flawless perfect landing.

She risks it all for her show, and oh, our smile!

E bb Demont

1

968, I'M SURE IT WAS, late summer of 1968.

I had been flying my Parks P-2A biplane around the Midwest, hopping passengers from farm fields, when I got a call from Billy Howe. He lived in Pennsylvania, an airplane pilot, a dealer in antiques, and he owned the only other flying P-2A in the world.

So began a fine friendship.

I flew to meet Billy and his wife at a small grass-strip airport not far from Wilkes-Barre. They took me to their home, the Howes leading the way as we entered.

From the front door a hallway led to the living quarters, a hallway mounted with antiques that Billy had collected: a Kentucky Standard rifle, a kitchen artifact, a painting or two.

" . . . and in this room," Billy was saying from the end of the hall, "is this quilt, which as best I can tell was made in 1720, maybe 17– . . . Richard?"

He had noticed that he was talking to himself. For I had stopped halfway down the corridor, transfixed at the sight of a painting, eye-level on the wall.

He retraced his steps. "Richard?"

His voice sounded as if he were speaking from the bottom of a well, a hundred feet down.

The face in the painting! I know that man!

"Billy," I whispered. "Who is this person?"

"Richard, you're white as a sheet! Are you feeling . . . "

"Who?"

"Well, I'll tell you who." He lifted the painting from its place on the wall. "It's on the back, as I recall. Yes. Look here."

I looked.

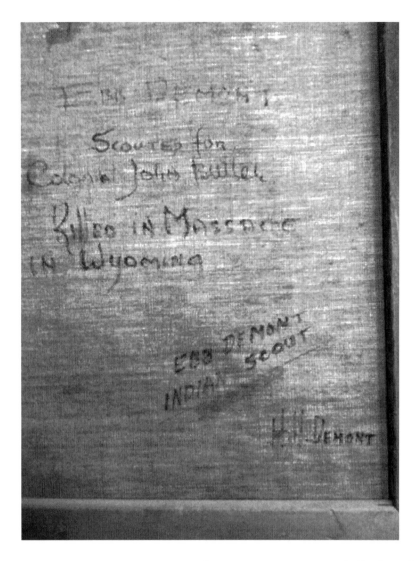

I heard my own voice raging, denying. "He wasn't killed! Billy, he wasn't killed in that massacre!"

Billy looked at me. "If you say so, Richard. But it says right here . . . "

"He wasn't killed!" I knew I had raised my voice, I was nearly shouting in my friend's quiet home. I sensed that Mrs. Howe, in the other room, might be wondering why she let this man into her house.

I've heard of such things, accounts by others recognizing faces in old paintings. This was the first and only time it happened to me. I had either known Mr. Ebb Demont as a dear friend, or I had been Demont himself. I was outraged, that someone had written that he was killed, when he hadn't been killed at all!

Billy didn't remark that I must be insane. He talked me down with history.

"The Wyoming Massacre wasn't in Wyoming, Richard. It was in the Wyoming Valley, here in Pennsylvania. 1778. Not all that far from here, as a matter of fact, west of Wilkes-Barre. The British, with a band of Indian warriors . . . the American settlers, and some militia went to fight them . . . "

"He was not killed." It was the only thing I could say. It was all I knew.

I shook my head, several times, Billy finally walked me away from the portrait. We talked about airplanes. I flew home. I forgot.

A year later, bad news. Billy Howe was killed in a mid-air collision, the Cub he was flying struck from above and behind by a faster modern aircraft.

I wrote a letter to Mrs. Howe, the best words I could find.

Five years later, it crossed my mind: Ebb Demont. I called Billy Howe's widow.

"Do you remember that painting in your hallway?"

"The Indian Scout? Of course I remember. I remember you and Billy talking about it."

She meant me shouting, but chose to be kind.

"Is there any chance that painting might be for sale? I had the most . . . you know I had a rather strange attr . . . "

"It may be for sale, Richard. I sold it to a dealer last year."

Oh, my. "Do you remember the name of the dealer?"

"I do. I've sold him quite a number of antiques."

In ten minutes I was talking with the dealer. "Oh sure, the Scout. I remember that well. I sold it a few months ago . . . "

Oh, my. "I wonder, sir, would you consider giving the buyer a call, tell them you have a customer who will buy it back, at any price?"

"At any price?"

"Yes sir. You see that painting is important to me . . . " I told him the story.

Two months later the painting was hanging on my wall. I flew to Wilkes-Barre, found that the Historical Society had lost hundreds of books and records in the flood two years before.

There was no reference to Demont, Ebb or otherwise, Scout

or otherwise. But I learned more than I wanted about the Wyoming Massacre.

There were two Colonels Butler at the battle, one American rebel and one British, "kin," according to one account.

The American Colonel Zebulon Butler was part of the defeated, although he survived. If Ebb Demont scouted for Colonel John Butler at the Wyoming Valley, he was scouting for the British and the Indians, he was on the side that was doing the massacre.

Two of John Butler's scouts were killed that day, unnamed by history. Depending on the account, between 227 and 400 Americans were killed, in a battle that became a rout. Most of the county was abandoned for years after.

Maybe the painting is fiction. I hope it is. It feels strange even today, when I walk by Ebb Demont's portrait, when I glance into those blue eyes looking back on me.

I know that man. He wasn't killed.

*I*nterview: Iran Part I

THIS INTERVIEW is still in the midst, I'm still thinking and editing even after answering the questions, treating a quick talk as though it were a chapter in a book. Here it is, mid-process, still changing. For some reason the edit feature has gone a little squirrely, so please forgive the strange formatting, misalignments, etc.

With Alireza Bahrami, www.thinkplus.ir

Dear Mr. Bach, this is my first question: Use three sentences to introduce yourself.

1) Hi.

2) Please call me Richard.

3) You'll recognize me as a mirror of yourself, having made different choices in the belief of time and space to express the shared truth of our spirit and of the love that binds us beyond space-time as indestructible Life.

****

Question #2: *Which one do you like more to be known as, and why: Richard Bach, the writer, or Richard Bach, the pilot?*

I'll pick Number Three, please: Richard Bach, temporary mortal, permanent spirit.

The spirit knows it flies (as it likely does every night in sleep); the mortal hammers a machine that can lift from the earth with his own body aboard, and begins to follow.

The spirit knows who we are and why we're here; the mortal strives for the pleasure of remembering this, connecting with other spirits in the midst of all our tests and challenges: Don't worry, we're here to practice becoming the highest Us we can imagine, in the midst of the thousand stones that would drag us lower.

Yet stones have only the power that we give them . . . we cannot be dragged, we cannot be separated, our truest selves, from an infinite Love that does not recognize us as mortal, ever, but as perfect Light from before the mist of time began.

****

Question #3: *If you get back to your teenage years, would you be proud of the adult person you now are? Why? / Why not?*

Does it make any difference how the teenage us would feel about the person we've become?

It does, if that teenager shares our motivations and goals, knows our values and why we act as we do. My teenager would think I'm a weird grownup because I don't celebrate birthdays. I'm weird to him because he doesn't understand the reasons why I don't do that.

By the time I explain to him the thinking behind every choice I make, he's grown up himself, he's me, and he understands completely.

I hope he understands, but more than that I hope he knows that we learn from experience, and that I've learned from events he's not yet lived.

If he's the kid I remember, he can probably accept that. If not, he'll find out soon enough.

On the other hand, I'm proud of him, for resisting peer pressure to be like all the other kids even when that pressure was awfully strong. I wouldn't be alive today, if it weren't for his choice to live by what he knew was right.

****

Question #4: *You are a famous pilot and your biography on Wikipedia shows you are a skillful one. How often do you fly in the sky of your imagination?*

I fly there every day. I fly there now, turning about its clouds and rainbows, finding answers to your thoughtful questions.

I plant questions like lightning-rods on the paths where I walk. Now and then comes a bright flash of sudden understanding . . . something that puzzled me, all at once I understand. The power of those flashes stays with me, and helps overcome tests I'll meet farther along my way.

True of all of us, I think . . . who among us does not spend time in the land of Wish and Dream? And bring those into the world of Make It Happen!

****

Question #5: *Is there any part of the world that you liked flying to but you couldn't? If yes, how do you feel about that area? (This question plays the role of a bridge, to bridge my last question to my next one.)*

Oddly enough, the answer is no. I've traveled a bit around the world, and wherever I've gone I've managed to find an airplane to fly. My journey has not been so much from place to place . . . that's a byproduct of the first journey, which is from the ground to the sky. That towering blue has become not a medium through which we fly but a pure destination of its own.

The kingdom of the sky, to me, is open wilderness, without borders. In some of its places lurk terrible dangers for mortals, storms to shear even strong aircraft, but wise pilots avoid those and for the most part the sky is a gentle land, a place of views and even ideas one doesn't meet on the ground.

In some lights, the shadow of one's aircraft on cloud is encircled by rainbows, as though the craft has become a spiritual creature itself, haloed in shimmering color.

Often, climbing away from a dark runway whipped in rain, one breaks out above the cloud—just a mile above the dark are drifts of bright marshmallow, of spun sugar and sunlight.

You have to love a calling which requires you carry sunglasses in your pocket when you start your engine and take off into a wicked black downpour. Like any wilderness, the sky is its own challenge and its own reward.

****

Question #6: *During our talks before the interview, you mentioned the term "worldwide family." Some members of this worldwide family live in Iran and are now reading this interview. Almost all of them are in search of success. Where and how can they find it?*

Success, to me, means I've reached some goal that matters to me. Those are almost always goals I've set for myself. Early on they were external: earn this pilot's certificate or that one, study and fly this airplane well, finish reading or writing this book or that one.

Those were important, and as I achieved those goals I felt successful.

As we grow, of course, we realize that since we're the ones setting, we can set any goal we wish. Some are difficult external challenges that may guarantee failure: Make Everybody Happy. Create World Peace. Eliminate Poverty.

Internal goals offer a different success: Make Myself Happy? I can do that! Am I becoming the person I decided to be? Day by day, I believe I am!

The answer for me has not been to change the outside world, but to create a geography inside that the outer cannot touch.

The more I study death and dying, for instance, a fascination of mine since childhood, the more I realize a strange thing . . . that what seems like awful death to observers is a beautiful moment for the one who's dying. Over and again those who have experienced a near-death experience report that they watched their body fall into death as they watched from a distance, pain-free, dispassionate at first and then becoming enveloped in joy and light.

The body is not who I am, they say . . . and it never was!

A similar event happened to me: as I slipped into a dream, my wife looked on my body in horror, convinced she was watching me die. After I came back she was left with a terrible memory of life extinguished. My recollection, of the same minutes, is sacred to me.

Our true life is indestructible by others, or even by ourselves. When we choose to believe this, and shift our goals to non-material events: to better recognize the spiritual world around us in place of the material appearances and seems-to-be, when we practice our ability to replace fear with understanding and love, no matter what appears to our eyes, we can feel our progress, day to day.

I have a long way to go to reach my own success at this. While I'm convinced that the whole material world is a game, it often happens that instead of rising above appearances with divine perspective I choose to play the game.

So I sigh, from time to time, and say that's OK, let the kid play his game, so long as there's a spiritual grown-up standing as guide:

"Don't take this life all so seriously, little one. Remember the wise Persian ruler, who wore his ring with the hidden reminder: *This too, shall pass away*."

And sure enough, the ring spoke true: he passed away, and his kingdom, as has every kingdom of the past and will every one of the future. Our greatest success comes from remembering who we are, everlasting spirit, not temporary biodegradable sculpture that moves and breathes for a few turns on the surface of this minor planet around its minor sun.

We can gain vast understanding in a single lifetime, when gaining understanding is fun for us, when we join the family around the world which plays this different game from all the rest.

When we choose to make that fun become our goal, that delight in discovery; when we learn perspective from our many triumphs and many disasters along the way, then we're found a success that no one can take but us, one life experience to the next.

****

Question #7: *The name of our website is "Positive Thinkers." In your opinion how can we live and think positively?*

The path that works for me is simple and wildly counter-intuitive: affirmation and denial.

We are every day presented with a million suggestions: loving uplifting positive suggestions as well as suggestions of fear and hatred, despair and destruction.

When I am alert, when I have the presence of mind to be aware that these are *suggestions* and not the truth of being, presented for my consideration, I respond to them for what they are.

I accept suggestions that I am creative and happy and glad for this opportunity to contribute to another's understanding or peace of mind or sense of well-being, and to my own.

I do not accept suggestions that I am sick or distressed or powerless, or that I am separated for an instant from the source of my being: absolute divine Love, unaware and uncaring of any suggestion that It does not exist, or that I am not Its perfect reflection.

Yes it feels odd, at first, when suggestion whispers, "Oh, you feel soooo poorly this morning! You must be coming down with an illness," it feels odd to deny it at once and affirm the opposite: "I am not feeling poorly at all! I am already in per-fect health, already at one with the center and circumference of my true being, which is perfect Love, and I shall not move from there!"

Feels odd, but it works. Those of us who practice this, we smile sometimes at just how well it works. "Resist the devil and he will flee from you."

Our devil is the suggestion that we are cut off from the Presence of Love, that we are cast adrift and alone in this harsh desert, subject to a million disasters.

"Resist . . . " and what felt like the beginning of illness is all at once gone, disappeared!

When we choose the opposite, accept the suggestion: "Oh yes, how true! I do feel awful today, and it's only going to get worse," guess what—it does.

It's not enough to simply deny the suggestions of the physical senses, at least for me, I need to affirm the spiritual opposite. Not only am I not-sick, I am perfectly well because I mirror forth my true being, which is always and ever well!

The statement, "Every day in every way I am getting better and better," is a fine beginning. We mortals are creatures of reason, too, so it helps to follow that affirmation: ". . . because I am already perfect Spirit, and it is my calling and destiny to show forth the power of Love wherever I turn my attention!"

Practicing affirmation and denial is a major, lifelong adventure.

Often I'll forget to use the tools I have at hand, I'll accept some false suggestion without thinking and have to battle my way back, denying in retrospect. There have been times I've used my affirmation constantly, every ten or fifteen seconds, over and over, for hours, until I am flooded with healing.

For every step backward we can take two forward, and see progress on our path to remembering who we are.

This way of thinking has been so fascinating to me that my last book, *Hypnotizing Maria*, turns around this idea that we have hypnotized ourselves, and we can de-hypnotize ourselves, as well. The book is even published in Farsi!

****

Question #8: *I like this sentence from "The Bridge Across Forever" which goes: For creating and bringing everything to your life, imagine that you have it now. Can you expand this sentence? Is it just the matter of imagination or other actions must be taken as well?*

The line in the original language is this: To bring anything into your life, imagine that it's already there.

It's well to question the phrase, "it's just imagination," with the implication that imagination is some frail wraith, powerless in real life.

Wrong! Everything we see about us, crafted at the hands of humans, was once imagination. The house we live in, the bed we sleep in, the airplane I fly, all were once a dream, were sheer imagination.

As the inventor does with thought, drafting and re-drafting her concept of a bridge which will one day appear as a sweep of iron, so do we with whatever we build in our own mind. We picture forth our desires and then go forth and do what we must to bring it into our experience, whether it be a home or a potato.

First must come an image of something we desire. Hold that image for long, actively decide, "That's for me!" then watch what happens. If our priority is strong and our creativity open, that which we visioned is moving closer, though for a while we may not see it as our mental warehouse-keeper dusts it off and hangs it on a rack for delivery.

Affirm it is already there, for it is. Then start your clock and look sharp.

****

Question #9: *Dear Richard I hope you are not tired of this 24-hour interview! This is my last question and then I am eagerly waiting for your own 2 questions.*
Please provide Positive Thinkers' viewers with some short talks which are directly related to them.

Short Talks directly related to Positive Thinkers:

You are the only hope for the future of civilization on the belief of this little planet.

The Negative Thinkers have their own future in mind, one of destructions, power-storms and despair for any but themselves.

Yet that future cannot be reached without the consent of others beyond themselves. The American President (or the so-called leader of any so-called nation) is incapable, for instance, of flying a warplane, or of commanding a ship of battle . . . he or she requires others, who do have those skills, to obey some command from above.

I wasn't aware of this until I sat in the cockpit of a military combat plane, years ago, three o'clock in the morning, waiting an order to launch on our targets. We didn't know whether the sirens that dashed us to our airplanes were simply another test of our reaction-time or a call to battle . . . this time it's real, guys!

In the hour in that red-lit cockpit, waiting to find out, I had a chance to think. My target, top secret then, was the railroad yard in Dresden. I had a map, but the headings and altitudes and turnpoints were memorized. If I weren't first blown out of the sky by a missile, I was ordered to destroy that target.

That's the first time I realized that if I did, it wasn't the President who would wake up screaming about the lives I had destroyed, or the innocents I would kill in the explosion of a bomb way too big simply to incinerate a railroad, but all the land around, all the people and their homes, their parents and their children, their tabby-cats and their Shetland Sheepdogs and their goldfish, their gardens and their memories and their wedding-plans for Sunday.

In that dark, my finger in easy reach of the Engine-Start button, I realized that the President is not responsible for my actions: I am!

The President, if he could look in my cockpit, he'd smile and say, "My, look at all those little dials and switches!" He'd have neither clue nor care of who I am, nor could he imagine that I have the power to withdraw my consent from his order to attack.

He is helpless to destroy, without me to do his killing for him! World leaders are free to say whatever they choose, free to lie when they feel that lies will sway others to join their paths to power. Without others to act as their knives, without me in my cockpit, world leaders are sad creatures, yearning to destroy, helpless to do so.

When that hour was done, a voice on the radio: "Alert terminated. Negative launch. Thank you, gentlemen."

Unstrapped from our aircraft, safety pins inserted once more in ejection seat handles and weapon fuses and landing gear, we rode silent back to our barracks.

Were the other pilots thinking the same as I had been—that each of us is responsible for every choice we make, and that we will bear the consequences of every one?

In politics or business, in art or in military, what's a Positive Thinker doing in the service of a destroyer?

My First Question for You, Ali:
What are the qualities and values that you believe most Iranians admire, and which define anyone that you and they consider an honorable, successful human being?

And my Second:
If you could speak to the whole world on behalf of yourself and your friends around you, what would you tell it, and us?

*I*nterview: Iran Part II

*O*NE OF MY REQUESTS to Alireza Bahrami when he asked for an interview was that I might be free to ask him two questions, myself. He consented.

RB: My first question for you, Ali—What are the qualities and values that you believe most Iranians admire, and which define anyone that you and they consider an honorable, successful human being?

AB: Happy New Year, Richard! In answer to your question, as I didn't want to scratch the surface of my beliefs and ideas, I fastened my seat-belt, closed my eyes and flew on the sky of my beliefs.

After a long deep contemplation which lasted twice the time you spent to answer the questions, I came to interesting conclusions which are happily shared with you and others.

Iranians admire he who tells the truth, at the times they feel telling lies is very widespread.

Iranians admire he who overcomes a difficulty, at the times they feel there is no other solution for that obstacle.

Iranians admire he who starts from the scratch, works his way and becomes successful and never cheats on the way.

A successful person is the one who knows who he is, what he wants, where he is, and where he wants to be. Someone who has the ability to have a pure life and tries his best when facing an obstacle.

I just checked Iranian Census Center's website. There are nearly 76 million people living in Iran and there are nearly 76 million answers to this question and I am sure Honesty is the mutual value among them.

RB: Second question: If you could speak to the whole world on behalf of yourself and your friends around you, what would you tell us?

AB: I like to tell everyone that we have come to Global Village, but our hearts are still far away from each other. Let's not judge and pre-judge about each other. Let's make our hearts close to each other by respecting each other and accepting others the way they are, not the way we want or like them to be. If so, that's when we can claim the real global village exists.

Dear Richard, all Positive Thinkers thank you for this great interview. I want to ignore clichés and ask you to finish the interview the way you like.

Warm regards,
Ali

RB: The way I'd like to finish our interview, at least for now, is to come back to where it started. The vast majority of us, no matter our nationality, are not monsters, one to another. Most of us of feel a deep respectful curiosity about those who dwell in different parts of the world: What have you learned that I need to know? What sets us apart, and more important, what are the values and principles that we share?

Yes, geography sets us apart, and language. And the power-seekers of every nation, for whom respect matters little, they set us apart, or hope to.

There are vast profits for them all, if only we agree that killing each other is infinitely more fun than caring and respect, and by the way don't we need to spend trillions of our dollars and our children's lives (not theirs), on the next-generation top-o'-the-line killing-machines?

Yet your answers suggest that we might pause, before pouring our blood and savings to yet another war, that we think a bit before listening to our power-elite, goading us into yellow fogs of fear and hatred.

Does it make sense, deep intuitive sense, to seek to destroy people whose values are the same as our own? For what you said so eloquently about Iranian values—you use the same words that so many of us Americans, and so many of every nationality around the globe, would use to paint our values, too!

Reflecting on that, personally, I'll choose to withdraw my consent, step back from fogs, from swamps of lies.

I'm not the only one with a stubborn streak: more than a few of us in America choose not to be manipulated by those who consider that we have become their personal property, that our minds are theirs to control, who have decided that they shall spin lies which we shall swallow and repeat.

Live by fear and hatred? We'll pass on that. We'd rather die.

(Dear Reader: The interview, and the entire website: www.thinkplus.ir, has disappeared.)

Searching the K

S HE ASKS TO BE ANONYMOUS, but what she sends is fascinating:

Dear Richard, This is an experience that I thought you would enjoy. Back around 2006 -2007, I and a couple of my friends became fascinated with the phenomena of Crop Circles. We emailed each other pictures of the latest designs appearing in fields around the world and perused websites for the latest findings.

"We discussed what we thought were causing these beautiful things to appear and their evolution from simple, rudimentary circles to complex geometric and alchemical designs. I suggested that the expansive media and internet coverage about them was directing more world-wide attention to the phenomena. In turn, that focus was bringing more Energy to the designs by the growing fascination with them by so many people.

"I proposed that I was going to try an experiment. I decided to meditate on a mental image of a Dragonfly appearing in a bright, green field. I did this only once, but could see it clearly.

"At the end of the following crop circle season (they tend to appear in Spring and Summer), I checked the websites for a Dragonfly design, but none appeared. I got busy with life, traveling with my job and pretty much forgot about it all.

"Last evening, I watched a documentary on Netflix streaming called, "Crop Circles: Quest for Truth." It was a very reasoned study of the phenomena over the last 30 years and the quest for finding the origins of the phenomena. After watching it, I was intrigued again, and decided to look on the Internet for the latest crop circle pictures. Lo and Behold, there was a picture of a Dragonfly Crop Glyph that appeared in a field in Wiltshire, England in June, 2009!!! Lovely!

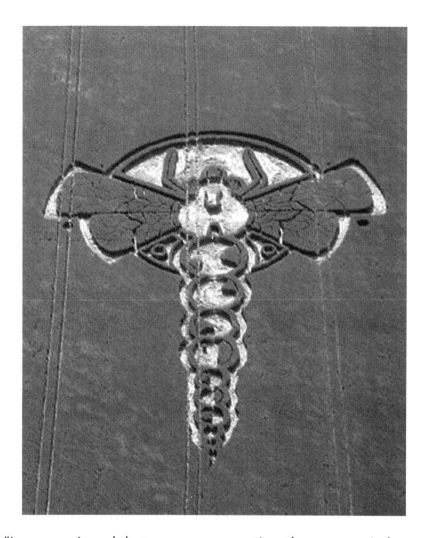

"I am convinced that we are co-creating these crop circles with a Higher Source of Energy (no, not aliens) and that it is a very benevolent and supportive guidance awakening us to our potentials. The Great IS is letting us know that our thoughts do manifest things.

"Therefore, it would be wise and much more fun, to manifest what we want in our physical adventure, than to concentrate on what we do not want or what we fear.

"Perhaps, It is also letting us know there is nothing to fear. What better proof than this that we are so much more than what we think we are? I have attached a picture of my Dragonfly for you to see. If you share this on your website, please omit my name. I tend toward the solitary and anonymous, and enjoy it immensely.

"Interesting things are unfolding for us all and I believe this is going to be a year of real awakening. I, for one, am enjoying the ride!

****

—Thank you dear Anonymous! You are so right, "interesting things are unfolding."

I went to my big book of Crop Circle photos, turning pages, asking, Could these have been co-created, some sort of mental/spiritual other-dimensional aspect of our own natural power to shape appearances in space-time?

Are we singing to ourselves, what is our music telling us, and equally important, what kind of spirit, who among us, is choosing to listen?

We who are drawn to a symphony or a rock concert or an air-show, we all share at least one sensitivity, one central desire in common. Is there some meta-mathic K, some constant in the equation between the transmitters of the crop circles and us fascinated receivers of their wonder-full mystery?

If so, what would you guess that constant might be, and what's the reason it's manifesting today?

$\mathcal{G}$lossary

$\mathcal{T}$HIS IS SIMPLE stuff, but there's a place for simple in our lives. Expect this will be added to, along the way.

Good: That which makes us happy.

Bad: That which makes us unhappy.

Evil: That which makes us extremely unhappy.

Guilt: The tension we feel to change our past, present or future for someone else's sake.

Happiness: A sense of well-being.

Meaning: That which changes our thought, and therefore our lives.

Philosophy: A way of thinking about the universe that guides us in daily life.

Prayer: The conscious grateful understanding that we already have all we need, and that nothing can separate us from the source and principle of our being.

Religion: Our way of finding what is true about the universe.

Selfish: Acting in our own long-term best interests.

Truth: That which we accept as valid.

There's Probably Some Explanation

UT I DON'T KNOW what it is and maybe I don't care.

I wrote "Lucky and Me" a few weeks ago; on December 4, to be exact. I wrote:

"That's one way I'd describe my dog, too: Lucky the cool detached observer of the world around him, the way he watched the valley from his special spot on the ridge."

Then later in the story, when I was talking with the animal communicator after Lucky died, she said, "I'm supposed to tell you he had a spot outside where he would just want to lay there and observe, like a lookout. To tell you sometime you can see him there. It's not your imagination—if you haven't seen him, you will."

I've looked at Lucky's observation spot from time to time since then and so far it's been quiet and empty. It may be years before I see him there, but I'm pretty sure that some day I will.

The funny thing, though, and what I can't explain, is this: I turned on my computer yesterday and went into iPhoto as I often do, and noticed an odd thing. Under "RECENT" was the date "June 6, 2011."

That's not recent, I thought, that's six months ago. Curious, I clicked on the date and here's what happened:

There are 949 pictures in my iPhoto section, hundreds more
Recent than June 6, 2011.
Why that particular photo of Lucky, all of a sudden, filling the
screen the instant I clicked the date-tag?

I can't figure this one out.

Do I want to?

$\mathcal{R}$arely Asked Questions: Lots of Mail?

$\mathcal{I}$ DON'T QUITE UNDERSTAND what goes on with writers and reader mail.

Every once in a while there's a news story about the loads of mail that come to one author or another, mailbags full of letters.

Sometimes in my computer I hear, "I know you get a lot of mail."

Not true. I'm busy with other things, but not with letters in my mailbox. That mailbag-on-the-desk is so not-me that I wonder if the stories are press releases and the photos fake. Yet they must be true . . . where would one find a mailbag stuffed full of letters for the camera?

If my publishers forward three letters in a month, that's a flood of mail for me. The average month is zero. I've told them to return unopened any manuscripts or envelopes bigger than letter-size, but I didn't ask them not to forward any mail at all.

So what, since I probably won't answer letters anyway? (I read them, and intend to answer, but then life crowds into my barely organized world and I hope the senders know that I appreciate their words even if I don't respond.)

So what? So it reminds me that the family of readers of my books is 1) small, and 2) the sort who feel it isn't necessary to send mail to those who write books. I like both.

I never write to authors. Almost never. I have written one letter to an author my life long, and that one was to Ray Bradbury, in 1963.

He answered!

Mr. Bradbury was so organized.

*W*hat's It All About?

*E*ASY TO REMEMBER, the time in my life when that was a towering question.

Yes there were beautiful places, lovely days, but there were storms and depressions, too, solid things torn from the earth and scattered by winds. One pretty sunrise, and then another storm!

What am I doing here and if it's supposed to be for the love of God, why don't I feel that and why am I on this God-forsaken planet?

Those were the days when I was doing exactly what I needed to be doing, asking that life-turning riddle, tested as I recall by not just one but about three thousand events that I perceived as Negative, all in a row—menial jobs, low pay, rejection slips, the car repossessed. Oh, wait. There was the pretty sunrise. Fourteen hundred disasters, one fine sunrise, sixteen hundred more disasters.

The disasters weren't all violent (some were), they were most of them barnacles grown on my sleek hull, cutting a few tenths from my cruising speed, then a few tenths more, empty So-Whats piling one on the other till I was dead slow in the water.

What I was missing all that time, simple thing that the one sunrise offered, was perspective.

I was seeing this:

While above and all around is this:

Like most of us slow learners, it took me a while to get my head out of the trees, to stop thinking of myself as the ant lost in a forest.

As I am a particularly slow learner from way at the back of the bus, I needed special help. Without knowing reasons, I chose coincidences that led me to flying. Only much later would I discover why I felt intense love for something I had never done and for which no one in my family or even in my acquaintance cared a fig.

Because they didn't need what flying offered and I did: perspective. I needed actual perspective, to perch on clouds hour after hour and then let go, turning this way and that, climbing till even cloud canyons became trifles below.

I needed to see with my eyes, literally, that what's a Big Deal on the ground is nothing . . . it is nothing! from the air.

The shout of my pals: "I'm goin' out and gettin' drunk tonight!"
That had zero charm, that meant zip next to the sound of
an airplane engine, firing into life, the blast of it going full
throttle, an airplane launched down the grass and over the
trees, into the sky.

Over the trees!

At last, from altitude, the world began to make sense. This
planet's a speck of dust. It's a pretty speck of dust, all right,
but no way is this place my home. This feeling I don't belong
here, it's true. I don't belong here!

Then why . . . ?

Because I can test myself here, and I can't do that at home!

At home we don't have beliefs we're separated from Love,
beliefs we're struggling faltering mortals, stumbling out of
our cradles thrashed about by hurricanes and flying debris
slammed against something sharp and thence into our grave
end of pointless story.

Lucky us, on this planet, we do have these beliefs! And as far
as we know, everybody has same belief so it must be true,
so I must be wrong about there's a reason I'm here there's a
reason for every single testing event of my lifetime, that must
be wrong.

And the reason, smart-guy future-me who's learned What It's
All About, the reason is . . . ?

To overcome the appearance that we're powerless! And you know what, kid-that-I-was-(and-whom-I-still-love-no-matter-you're-sometimes-clueless)?

Overcoming that appearance, showing, demonstrating who we truly are beneath our helpless seems-to-be is more fun than . . . it's more fun than flying airplanes!

What's the very first thing you learned, flying. The first thing?

I'll trust what I cannot see?

RIGHT! Toss the kid that teddy-bear-with-scarf-and-flight-jacket!

There's a principle, lad, a Principle that you cannot see, just like the Aerodynamics you cannot see, and that Principle brings you impossible coincidences to lead you all the way through life, so long as you find who you want to be—who you want to pretend to be because your real self is so far beyond pretend you can't even glimpse . . . closest you can come is maybe fire from a cutting torch on steel two inches from your black goggles and then throw the goggles off . . . that light is who you are!

Every day, every second you're on this planet you're free to forget your light, to stuff it away.

You're free to think you're one of seven billion here and everybody else is better'n me and smarter and richer and luckier and privilegeder than me. Absolutely free. Free to kill yourself if you want and nobody can stop you till you're back in light and you remember: I chose my tests because I knew I could pass 'em!

Not only knew I could overcome whatever test I threw at me, it'd be so much fun to do it that I picked this lifetime for the sheer joy of proving who I am in the middle of what everybody else thinks is impossible!

This world is a game, Neo. You don't think you know the rules, but you know the rules.

Rule Number One: Remember it's a game! It seems real because the game's no fun if it's easy, if it's clearly a game that ten-story building's just cardboard. That building's got to weigh a million tons, seem like the real thing.

No game's fun if you can't lose (forget you can't really lose no matter what because your home's not here, it's on a dimension around here but you mustn't know that at first you have to discover it for yourself along your way, in the middle of some hurricane).

All the rest of the rules you know. You think you don't know but you know.

What's it all about?

It's about remembering, dear kid. Remembering that you are no more kid than I am. Remembering that you and I are Light, playing at darkness: Oooooh, isn't the darkness scary?

Well?

Isn't it?

*R*arely Asked Questions: Still skydiving?

*N*OPE, NOT any more.

One summer, typical obsessive me, I decided to overcome my fear of heights (in fact, my fear of falling great distances and meeting the ground at high speed).

Because I always like getting through the Newcomer phase quickly, I made seven jumps that first day of training, out of static-line phase into free-fall by sunset. In the next few months I made 51 jumps.

I was still shall we say alert, standing in the wind on that last step outside the airplane as we approached the drop zone, as though aware that I had not chosen the world's most forgiving sport to romance at that point in my career.

The other jumpers, as far as I could tell, had long since gotten over that awareness. Relaxed and confident, they'd practice somersaults alongside me in free-fall, then go vertical and blaze downward, away from my stable spread-eagle security-blanket.

When we'd break away after joining for a while a five- or seven-person star, I'd be keenly interested in finding a place to pull my ripcord that didn't happen to be directly under someone who hadn't. Not that the other jumpers didn't do the same, I was unhappy for not being as comfortable with the routine as they were.

Around my 48th jump, I did a silly thing. (That's an ominous sentence, isn't it?) I didn't check to see that all the straps on my harness were every one of them securely tucked in, so they couldn't flail around in the slipstream as I fell, and so offer a one-in-a-thousand chance for the pilot chute to snag and catch, a second after I pulled the D-ring.

When this happens, I found, time slows way down. Instead of the sudden wrenching jar of of good opening, I felt a gentle slowing. I looked up and saw, instead of a nice inflated square canopy overhead it looked like colored trash-bags flailing, calling down to me, "This doesn't seem natural to us, Richard. Does it seem natural to you?"

I wrote about the event *in The Bridge Across Forever*: that meeting with the observer riding on my shoulder, grading me harshly for not analyzing my situation correctly, for not realizing that even after I cut away from the rag of the main canopy, the wreck was still tied to me by the fouled pilot chute, and for pausing a while remembering my training: never open a reserve parachute into a fouled main canopy.

By the time I realized that it might be better at least to try the reserve than to hit the ground at my current airspeed, I was earning low grades indeed, from my observer. But sure enough, I lucked out.

The reserve opened a few seconds before my boots hit the grass. I still have that D-ring and ripcord cable, by the way.

Just to prove I hadn't been emotionally crippled by Jump Number 48, I repacked and took off for Jumps 49 through 51.

It was in the freefall on 51 that I remembered about my reserve opening . . . I had lucked out. There had been an even chance that the reserve would itself have fouled, caught in the wreck of the main canopy, and I would have squashed bug-like on windshield Earth.

Upon reflection, after landing, I discovered that I preferred not to have my life depend on lucking-out. If my lack of skill runs out and I bend an airplane, that's my responsibility and my consequence. If I run out of luck it's a different story. Not acceptable.

Captain Chicken, after a long battle, prevailed. I returned to flying airplanes and gliders and paragliders and helicopters and antiques and seaplanes, single-and multiengine machines that didn't require a reserve parachute (except for the paragliders, of course, and that education ended not from a near-death experience, but from a dearth of local launch-sites, from the boredom of para-driving hundreds of miles in an automobile only to find that the wind at the new site was from the wrong direction).

Seaplanes. That's what it is today, and it has been for a decade or so. Nothing, can possibly go wrong, in a seaplane (so long as I check at least ten times that all wheels are UP before landing on the water, all wheels are DOWN before landing on the runway. This check does not depend on luck).

I am such a chicken.

Happy little chicken.

"*Mesdames et messieurs les voyageurs...*"

I HEARD IT, boarding the train from Chaumont to Paris. This was a while ago, and I thought no more than the wisp of a smile at the conductor's voice in the speakers: "Bonjour mesdames et messieurs les voyageurs . . ." The rest of the announcement was in French, so I didn't understand a word.

But it struck me then and it strikes me now, piling into bed at 1 am with my computer and no reason to remember. What a thoughtful elegant way to begin a travel! We passengers weren't cattle crushed into a boxcar, harried about with our rush and our disparate concerns. We were *voyageurs*, we were ladies and gentlemen, citizens of an honorable country, and wherever we planned to visit we'd bring our civility and justice and respect for the rights of others.

I had been ennobled by a phrase.

There are few modern cultures much suited to taking over the world. Give me a minute, I can't think of one. But since somebody has to do it, I'd prefer it be the French.

At least the world will be taken gently, with charm and courtesy. It's true, isn't it, that the French invented *courtoisie* in the thirteenth century, when everyone else was running around hitting people with sticks?

Yes. I checked. It was the French

Do we need to vote on this, or do I just hope they take over on their own?

Yesterday's Coincidence

IN MY FIRST book, *Stranger to the Ground*, I wrote as a pilot who flew a warplane with the white star of the U.S. Air Force on its wings. On those pages I wondered about the men who fly on the other side of the then-Iron-Curtain, the ones just like me but who flew with red stars on their wings.

"If war is declared," I wrote, "I will have lost the host of unmet friends who are the Russian pilots." And a bit more of how I felt closer to these who fly because they love flying than I feel to my own countrymen, Americans who shout hatred toward them.

That feeling's never faded, but I had no voice, there was no way I could say it to those men and women themselves.

Imagine my surprise, a few years ago, when a box, travel-battered, return address missing, arrived in the mail. No note inside (it may have fallen out through one of the holes in the package). Just this:

to Richard D. Bach
from Russian Pilots
Moscow, 2007

Little-Known Excerpts:
(From: "Running from Safety")

WE MUST HONOR our dragons, encourage them to be worthy destroyers, expect they'll strive to cut us down. It's their duty to ridicule us, it's their job to demean us, to force us if they can to stop being different! And when we walk our way no matter their fire and their fury, our dragons shrug when we're out of sight, return to their card games philosophical: "Ah, well, we can't toast 'em all . . ."

[**NOTE:** I thought Little-Known Excerpts was a good idea. It is a good idea and I'll find more of them. But the price! I had to open *Running from Safety* to find that quote, and after I copied it down, I looked for others and the whole book is full of 'em! I forgot that book is amazing honey-to-bee powerful for me. I fell into the pages and didn't come out for half an hour.

Well, it's your own book! You ought to like it, Richard!

Sure, and yes it was a bestseller for a while but if you enjoy messing with ideas, though, it is really some neat book!]

—Next day—

From *Hypnotizing Maria*, this little mantra I think about some-times once a week, sometimes (when I'm in the-belief-of-trouble) every few seconds, over and over again:

"I am a perfect expression of perfect Love, here and now. Every day I am learning more of my true nature, and of the power I have been given over the world of appearances. I am deeply grateful, on my journey, for the parenting and guid-ance of my highest right."

Depending on the nature of my challenge, for "perfect Love" I'll say, "perfect Life," or "perfect Spirit." I say the whole thing fast the first time, then go back and think about it, remember incidents and examples of times I've used that power over the world of appearances, remember that I'm being led even this moment, through whatever my test may be.

After I'd been doing this for a year or so came the first time I truly made the shift, switched my concept of my identity from spirit-using-a-body to my highest self, itself! I'm not just a lesser being that my highest self is helping along the way, I am that self!

I know that from other perspectives, what I see as higher self is still a limited expression of a formless Higher. But hey, step by step is not all bad!

—Next day—

Note of Interest: There's a section in *RFS*, five or six pages
so too long to insert here: a talk with a boyhood friend that
stayed with me all this time. The book uses his real last name,
but when we were ten years old and we were best friends he
wasn't Anthony, he was Budgie. Then he moved away I didn't
know where.

Missing him, thirty years later, I wrote a story for *Family Circle*,
called *Budgie Zerbie, Where Are You?* (I spelled his last name
phonetically so it would pronounce right.) In the story I wondered about our childhood friends who disappear from our
known world, where were they today, did they think of us as
we think, from time to time, of them?

Not long after the story was published I got a telephone call.

"Hullo," I said.

"Dickie? Is this Dickie Bach?"

I knew right away. Not just the name he called me, it was his
voice. I guess we never forget voices. *"Budgie!"*

We see each other from time to time to this day, still best
friends.

You've probably heard his voice, too. Google Anthony Zerbe.

I *Love It When I Solve Ancient Mysteries*

*T*HE CONTROVERSY began in the 14th century, I believe, and it was a big one:

How many angels can dance on the head of a pin?

To the best of my recollection, the heads of pins were some-what larger, seven hundred years ago, but the question raged even as the area of a pinhead's real estate decreased.

It raged in me, till this evening. I hadn't personally wrestled with the question since 1976, but my secret problem-solver never gives up on a case, and she just tiptoed into my study, set the answer on the corner of my desk, and tiptoed out, a glad little smile at the corner of her mouth.

QUESTION: How many angels can dance on the head of a pin?

ANSWER: How many angels can dance on the point of it?

I read that, printed with her fourteenth-century calligraphic quill, the letters of the word "ANSWER" illuminated in scarlet and indigo and gold leaf upon her parchment, and all my Tensions Over Unanswered Questions regarding angels and pins, they disappeared.

If fewer angels can dance on the point than on the head of the pin, then the angels, no matter their size, are constrained by space and time and therefore the answer will be "–n– angels can dance thereupon," and the ballroom doors be closed to others.

If on the other hand the same number of angels can dance on the point as on the head of the pin, then angels are not con- strained by spacetime, and an infinite number of impatient angels Oh! so tired of waiting to party, have plenty of room to kick up their heels at last, and polka non-stop through eter- nity.

The issue, praise be, is resolved. There'll be a secret bonus by somebody's work station tonight.

That Which Makes Me Happy

THIS IS A STORY of so-called good and pretend evil.

You don't have to be a chess-player to study the picture and know it's a battleground. You know by the nature of human beings that our games require winners and losers, the victors and the defeated. So many of our sports are meant to be showcases of skill, tests to display the beauty of superior skill.

They do this, yet almost always there's a final scene, half triumph half disaster.

Knowing this we can see that the game above was not going well for White. Look at the row of its captured pieces, lifted off the board, at the far side of the photograph. For proof, instead of holding its own, White has taken only three of the opponent's pieces, and is being ravaged on this side of the board by Black, who has swept down to dominate the game.

And yet, when we look way in the corner at the far right side of the board, we see that White has pulled off a miracle. His Queen's flown to storm the very bedchamber of Black's King, who cannot escape, and the game is over.

Victory goes to battered White.

Good for White! The underdog, the Rocky Balboa of this game, flashing in what must have been a stunning surprise, from collapse to victory.

Now study this next view of the same board . . . all I did was walk round the table and snap the picture from the other side:

On this side are lined the trophies of Black's battles won. That's a long line of White's forces, or former forces, in the Great Hall of the Black King, nearly three times as many pieces gained than lost. Yet for all the trophies, all its battles won, the war for Black ends in defeat. Bad for Black.

And there you have it. Triumph and Disaster, Good and Bad expressed on one board, 64 squares on a tabletop.

The principle's the same when the chessboard's a thousand miles wide, or the surface of the planet.

I was a child during the Second World War. I remember newspapers filled with diagrams of battles on the European front, the North African front, the South Pacific, the North Atlantic.

355

When the Allies (Us) won a battle, there was rejoicing . . . what good news! When we lost, our armies captured or destroyed, our territories overwhelmed by the Axis (Them) . . . those were bad days. Are we at the end of the world? No one knew how the war would end, and some of us kids were scared.

And yet, even as a child, I knew that every defeat that made us unhappy: the fall of France, of Corregidor, the victories of the Luftwaffe in Poland and the Low Countries, of the Afrika Korps in Tobruk, of the Japanese Navy at Midway, these same defeats of the Allies were celebrations, champagne and confetti for the soldiers of the Axis.

What was Bad for us, the very same outcome, it was Good for them.

You lose, I win: Good for me, Bad for you.

You win, I lose: Bad for me, Good for you (damn you to Hell).

Being slow to learn, it took me several decades to reach the conclusion that an important discovery had been made.

It isn't just battles, it's Everything.

By definition. Good is that which makes me happy; Bad is that which makes me unhappy. One becomes the other when we rotate the board, change me from Black at one side of the board to White at the other.

Variations are small talk about intensity. Wonderful! is what makes me Very Happy. Evil is what makes me Very Unhappy.

Human sacrifice, for instance, it's an evil thing to most cultures, since most of us abhor pointless deliberate murder of the innocent.

A different culture, though, values human sacrifice, be it virgins to the gods or suicide-bombers to political causes. Human sacrifice isn't murder, it's a privilege! It's not just good, it's wonderful to die for a cause higher than ourselves.

Try it this minute, a thought-experiment. Can you name anything that makes you truly happy which you believe is Bad? Or anything that makes you truly unhappy, which you call Good?

I'm talking about you, now, your own life, not what you imagine a serial killer or Godzilla-on-the-rampage may think.

It took me a while, but at last I wrapped my mind around it. This planet is a spherical chessboard, the stage for our games of Good and Evil, from personal jubilation and bad-hair days to global healings and mass destructions.

Does our belief in a benevolent God make us happy? Good. Does our belief in a cruel God or an uncaring, who sends destruction or is powerless to stop it, does that make us unhappy? Bad.

My personal choice, bouncing off both, is to exchange a mortal God for a Principle of Love, divinely indifferent to our beliefs of life in spacetime. That Love knows only its own perfect spiritual Self, and us as perfect reflection, here and now.

Our dreams and adventures in limitation? The Principle doesn't care what we dream about our separation from It, about mortal bodies, justice and injustice, living and dying, joy and sorrow—it is The Is, and we are one with It.

This belief makes me happy. I do my best to practice remembering, on my bad hair days, that divine Love won't notice I'm wearing a hat. It makes me happy, and that's Good.

Be careful, kids, reading newspapers.

$\mathcal{Z}$ sa-Zsa, on Her Walk

$\mathcal{E}$ VERY MORNING, every afternoon, Zsa-Zsa the Sheltie and I go for our walk. If it weren't for that little sheepdog, I'd probably drive.

But she takes her job as Personal Trainer seriously, and now that Lucky is researching his different dimensions, it's ZZ's bark that tells me it's time to close the computer and get a few miles under our paws!

She's convinced that a walk's our cure for every physical ill, for loneliness, for thinking too much, which is not dog-friendly activity.

She's had an up-hill battle on that subject with me: thinking too much. Actually not an up-hill battle, today, but a down-hill one. She caught me lost in thought on our walk this afternoon, so when she barked to say what a beautiful day! I realized I had come to a stop, looking at the ground. Here's what I saw at my feet:

Do you notice anything revealing about that photo? I didn't, and then the ZZ barked again, "Look!" so I blinked, and saw this:

What she was suggesting, whilst she pretended to look in a different direction, was that perhaps by staring preoccupied at the ground I was missing something important on my path. Do you see them, the marks of a tracked vehicle, throwing shadows on the roadway ahead?

There was a pattern, directly in front of my eyes, but by concentrating on the minutia of my close-up view, I had been blind to what it was telling. Oh, now when I look at the close-up photo, I can see a bit of the pattern even in the detail, but I couldn't see it before till I stood back and found a little perspective.

Once seen, of course, the pattern's obvious: Something powerful went this way, and in using its power to gain the traction it needed to continue, it changed the road itself, left a print of that change for anyone following to see.

"Don't you think that's us, too, Richard?" Zsa-Zsa trotted back to me, stood near. "That we need to see patterns in our paths, too, sometimes patterns that no one else can see, and as we dig in to follow them, we leave the tracks of our own cycles of challenge and reward, failure and success?

"We can fail to see," she said, "preoccupied with our own concerns, but when we choose to claim our perspective, notice what's been in front of us all along, we'll find stories of determination and success in the very dust of the ground, every story singing to us along our way.

"Do you notice, too, the end of that track on the road? For all its grappling and wresting with the physical world, the track fades out, downhill, almost as though the track-maker, earning a miracle, gently lifted into the air and left the earth."

Zsa-Zsa looked up, held her gaze on me. "Look sharp, master," she said. "That's your path here, and mine, the path of all us mortals. We wrest with spacetime, striving for traction, for meaning to it all. Finding it, whether we notice or not, we've left our patterns for others to consider along the road. And then we lift free, taking our lessons with us as we go."

That's my dog Zsa-Zsa. I wonder if now and then, for all her insisting otherwise, that puppy thinks too much.

I must take her for a walk.

*R*arely Asked Questions:
Did Illusions Really Happen?

*Y*es, it happened. No, it didn't.

The book *Nothing by Chance* is a straightforward non-fiction account of a summer in the biplane (with photographs), flying through the Midwest, hopping passengers from small-town hayfields, three dollars the ride.

A few years later we flew the adventure again (with more biplanes) for a documentary film of the same title. All of that "happened," that is, we can find records here and there to confirm that others noticed, were changed and affected by the flying machines and the cameras and the crowds coming to watch.

There are photos in newspaper archives, pictures in scrapbooks through Nebraska and Iowa, Illinois and Wisconsin and Missouri. Land in those fields today, you'll see the scrapbooks for yourself.

Into such events flew Donald Shimoda, nominated Savior of the World, who found the work not so satisfying as he had been led to believe. Turned in his keys, quit the job.

To the best of my knowledge Shimoda has never had a body in our space-time. That will make him, to many, someone who never really lived.

He really lived to me! Anyone's real who changes and affects the way we think and act and run our lives. No one can prove that Jesus the Christ had a body in space-time, or King Arthur . . . are these two dismissed as unreal?

What's real and what really happened, turns on our own personal definition. As I seek my guides and mentors, my examples of lives well lived, Did this person have a body? is so least-important on my list it's not even there.

I model my behavior on my highest sense of right, and that's built of encounters of spirit, no matter the touch of a so-called material world. Bethany Ferret, captain of the Ferret Rescue Boat Resolute, has shaped my code of conduct and ethic as much as Jesus has, probably more.

Bethany's real, and she lives in me. So does Jesus and Donald Shimoda, Tom Cutter and Constantine Shak Lin, Glenn Curtiss, Frank Tallman, John Gartner, Ray Bradbury and my own inner angels . . . they combine, all of them together, to make the semi-fiction person I am today, typing these characters one by one to a page that doesn't exist.

Am I real? Are you?

No, we're not. Yes, we are.

*F*rancais-faux et moi

*I*LOVE languages. I speak none of them.

It took me a while to realize that my American is a bit quirky to others.

I can get along in the language, pass as American, but when I start talking freely I lapse into Writer, splash about in colors instead of the better-understandable.

I'm careful, in some quarters, to say, "My, it's foggy!" instead of the more natural, "It's breathing marshmallows!"

Even when I write, there's a voice: "Careful now. Don't push words too far." You can imagine. Just the words to make me grab my paint-pot and set off running.

My high-school Spanish failed me in Madrid as I found that "Quiero te," to the waitress is preferred to, "Te quiero." But instead of killing me, she laughed. I learned a volume from that laugh.

Better learn French from just plain reading the language, figuring it out, I thought, instead of the agonizing declensions memorized, scores and hundreds of them. And look there; my machine doesn't have keys for the subscripts and superscripts, as if I knew what they are and where to put them.

So for the longest time I was stricken dumb by my conviction that whatever I said, I'd say it wrong.

Enter my Epiphany of the Day and thanks to the waitress: Who cares?

When I shifted places, when a French-speaker or a German does his best or her best to speak in American I can understand, I found that who cares about their grammar is not me.

"Go for it!" I say to my French acquaintance, my Spanish guest, "Just give 'er a try with the best English you can pretend, and leave the figuring-out up to me."

I understand, "Where are the boat to shore later?" well enough to point to the ferry-slip at the left and reply, "Ici, mademoiselle," or, "Alla, senor."

Then one day I realized that my own encouragements apply to me! When I do my best in another language, it's usually good enough that others know at least what I'm trying to say,

370

and they don't mind if I say it wrong!

So long as I give my disclaimer up front, most of my self-consciousness in speaking disappears.

I can be relaxed and shrug, "Je ne parle pas francais. Je parle francais-faux."

When I'm honest enough to admit that I only speak fake French, what're you gonna do, shoot me in my next word?

How did I learn fake French, fake Spanish, fake German, fake Esperanto?

Sheer vocabulary, no matter how limited. I learned them by picking up whatever words I could remember: bonjour, le chat, la or le table (in francais-faux it doesn't matter); caliente, pequeno, el perro (knowing I could say la perro and get away with it); autobahn, wie gehts, unmoeglich; Cu vi parolas Esperanto?

Then I merely use all the vocabulary I know with grammar I make up along the way based on American, fill in the blanks with imagined words and a flawless movie-accent: Alors, voila! Nous avons une opportunite' parlez avec pas de les grandes silences awkwardes quand je ne try pas communi-quez!

Eso es mucho mejor (al menos para mi), hablar en espanol-falso, que no hablar nada.

Und das ist besser als nichts, even wenn ich habe keinen deutsche Worten in Kopf sagen, und muss invente oder guesse an: "Wie schoen, das Pferd Ihr reitest heute, freulein!"

Of course it helps to memorize a line or two of the real stuff, in case one has occasion to quote something profound.

When that something also happens to meet my hope of the moment, I bend it to the situation: "Ayez l'oblegeance de me parlez avec douceur, sans levez la voix, et sans me contradire dans acune manier."

I use that quote often, and look, I can translate real French into fake Spanish: Habe Ud. la amabilidad de hablame sucretemente, sin llevando suyo voz, y sin me contradicto en cualquier manera."

It's a sentiment I often express to new friends in my own American: "Do me favor? Talk to me sweetly; never raise your voice to me, and never disagree with anything I say, OK?"

I don't know the characters for Wo sh'r iga hao pung yo, but I trust that this phrase will come in handy, explaining myself in Shanghai.

True, the superscripts can be devastating, I found: Diene Far spiese miene Blomster, depending on how I spell or pronounce that single Danish 'a' in Far, may be saying "Your father is eating my flowers," instead of what I mean: "Your sheep are." A critical difference for an oft-used sentence!

So yes, there are pitfalls. In St. Petersburg, my entire Russian vocabulary: "Moi brot advocat," mis-pronounced just a teeny bit, changes my assertion that my brother is a lawyer to the suggestion that he's an avocado. (I don't have a brother and he is neither a lawyer nor an avocado. I learned the sentence from a Russian book.)

I may get puzzled looks to my sentence, but if you were Russian, wouldn't you feel kindly toward a stranger who admits his relatives are unusual? Wouldn't you smile, and want to sort of look out for him during his visit to your country?

And besides, the implications of my sentence are wide. See what happens when I whisper or speak or shout my Russian sentence (using either pronunciation of advocat) to: the victim of a traffic accident;
> *a street vendor selling an innovative new gadget;*
> *a street vendor selling illegal drugs;*
> *a gentleman attempting a drugstore holdup;*
> *a lovely visitor from France, who speaks little Russian.*

Same sentence, so many meanings.

"Votre frère, monsieur," she replies, "il est une legume?"

Should this be her response, I'm prepared to shift at once from Russian into francais faux.

You know about me and So-What: Given all the foregoing, why do so many Institutions of Learning go to such massive painstaking agonizing lengths to teach perfect French to us blank-slate students; or flawless Spanish or impeccable High German?

With one result: That we walk away from four years of class terrified to utter a single word on the streets of Barcelona or Chaumont or Ingolstadt.

Unless we plan to become translators for the United Nations

Assembly, why not teach us (or hey, why not teach ourselves?) a mass of sheer vocabulary, index-card reminders taped to all the nouns in our home? Can we not be practical, please, and forget that sometimes it's "e" instead of "y" for "and" in Spanish?

No grammar at all, or just a taste, and let us get along very well, thank you, with our lingo infanto and a smile? It's a fact we have a family out there, and while they don't all speak our native tongue they're likely willing to dare ours if we dare theirs, a few words at least, for the fun of our hello.

"Oui, c'est triste, mademoiselle, la vie de mon frère. Mais moi, je suis pas d'une legume, je suis un homme merveilleux . . . "

When school kills (it does), and when it dies (it will), where's education?

I COULD PICK any country, but I'll pick the United States of America, because I've flown over it most of my life. But this flight, your permission, I'll do something different.

I've fit my flying goggles with these Mark IV Education Lenses. Invented by me. Look through the glass and see a quick green line for every person on the ground who has a college degree, a brown line for every other person, the un-degreed.

We see farther as we fly higher, of course, so let us cruise super high, for a biplane, way up at 11,000 feet.

(I hear the airline pilots snickering: " 'Way up at eleven thousand.' Oooh . . . that's really high! Snicker-snicker.")

Very well, you with the gold stripes on your shoulders, this is a thought-experiment, OK? Just sit there in the front cockpit for a minute and look out through your Mark Fours. I have something to show you!

Notice over the farmlands, we don't see a lot of green . . . not what you would call a forest of college-degree people, below. These are folks with different values from academics. A few emerald lines we see, then brown-brown-browns, hashmarks everywhere, like wheatfields in August.

Turn over a city, it greens up a bit. Swing over Microsoft country, or Cupertino, or Wall Street, the sight gets fairly lush in greens. Over Academia, of course.

Cruise back and forth over the land, though, fly straight-line coast to coast, turn round and fly back, we don't see a whole lot of mint-color, down below.

According to my goggles, the United States is mostly barren country, college degrees scattered, sparse.

I looked in a mirror through my goggles, by the way, and I'm the color of dead grass. Of course I am; dropped out of college first year, ran away to fly airplanes.

Now here's where it gets interesting. We're mid-air, I'm handing you a different set of goggles, my new Mark Five lenses. Look through these and now you see a green stripe for every soul who's free to educate herself himself on their own, set loose to follow their curiosities, whatever sings and drives their whim to discover, seizes their passion to know.

Now we're picking up old folks and young, all genders races religions philosophies backgrounds fears hopes determinations, anyone whelmed by the properties of wildflowers, or by sailing kayaks, or astronomy or dog-training or physics or math, and note that lady's struck with all these things and protozoology and praxeology and language modeling thrown atop.

Let's say these new green-lines don't care a fig for high-school diplomas or college degrees, say they don't need a Wizard of Awe to pronounce them educated.

But educated they are! Their diploma is the joy of understanding How It Works, What It Means, the power of So What to push their boundaries outward outward and outward again, day by electric day.

Then, don't you see: the deep vast infrastructurated human-resource of a whole nation has just this moment changed?

Keep looking, as we fly. What's the view now, hey? Look there! Where once was sere and desolate, the dead-grass failing chaff of school dropouts, now's gone green-laser lush below us, seething with living growing Self-Taughts, practicing experts discovering what no one has seen before, thought before.

All at once they're pouring the life of their discovery and invention into what we've been preached was a stagnant country, the death-pool of our Educated Society, the end of the world.
What have we done? What was our master stroke?

We ennobled "dropout," we redefined "education."
And with that stroke a country transforms from death and

stagnancy to roaring torrents of breakthroughs in science and invention, in philosophies and technology and sport and health—in all the fields once fenced about, gated and guarded and suffocated by self-conscious self-righteous for-profit Academia.

Did Bill Gates clutch some paper degree when he began his journey, did Steve Jobs, did Hobie Alter seek the blessing of a University, Doctor of Surfboard Engineering, to design his new-dimension boards and his Hobie Cat and his startling penguin-power kayaks, did Ray Bradbury spend one day in college before launching his writing career, did Thomas Edison's three months of formal schooling yield some parchment, essential in order that he change the world with his passion to know and to invent?

Negative, as we say in aviation.

I'm not suggesting we turn from learning or knowing or star-bright Education. I'm suggesting merely that we dump Formal Schooling, with its pricetags and its Greek societies, its drunken parties and its hand-in-hand pomposities, the somber gowns and useless hats. I'm suggesting we dump a cherished lie: we get this scrap of paper and now the straw we had for brains is all at once valuable.

In *Education and Ecstasy*, George Leonard distilled the research of his book into a single sentence. "Education, at best, is ecstatic."

Why ought anyone, why ought thee and me settle for education-at-worst, the droning of the uninspired herding the uncaring to a degree in the unnecessary?

Who knows better than we, where lies ecstasy? Who better than I, can tell me what fascinates my spirit, what it is that calls me while it calls no other? Where's the wisdom, trusting others to ignite some grand fire within myself?

I don't require a professor to tell me what I love, I already love it! The professor's job is to get his hell out of my way, to cease forever insisting that his memorized discoveries are Education and mine, spinning with delight, are paste.

What would our culture, what would our society be like today, if no one had a job, and everyone had a . . . Cross that out.

What would my life be like today, if I had no job, but a calling, instead?

What if what mattered more to me than anything was the sharing of ideas, was communicating whatever I've discovered that works for me, to those who matter to me?

Can I survive, selling what I've learned and done, invented and practiced, to others of like spirit? Could the gifts I find from my learning passions, wrought from my own personal private education unlike any on all the earth, could those be valuable to my little family around the world?

Sounds strange, impossibly idealistic. Yet isn't that the way that you and I are surviving today? Isn't each of us already:
offering something of value,
to someone who needs it,
who thanks us for it by paying us,
which helps us continue producing,
and meeting their needs?

Doesn't each of us pay something to someone who offers us some valuable idea or understanding, some service or commodity channeled through the person they have educated themselves to become?

George Leonard's book, for instance, came from his self-education about education. Is it worth its $12.95 cover price? No way, to anyone bored with ideas.

Worth every dime at ten times the price! to someone desperate to understand what education, set aflame by passion, might be.

The world's best book on how to educate ourselves, parchment-free, was published last year:

Secrets of a Buccaneer-Scholar, by James Bach.

The name's familiar to me, all right. The author dropped out of tenth grade, never went back to class, and became on his own the best-educated human being I've had the privilege to meet.

His book tells how he did it, how anyone can do it—James Bach translates Education and Ecstasy into nuts and bolts and every tool we need to make them fast.

A stagnant nation, despairing over the death of education . . . by the Great Cat, why? Have we not learned that school kills?

The nation ought to be raving joyful for the death of its failed system of diplomas and degrees, raving delighted at the greening of this grand new culture, the Passionate Self-Educated.

Put me in a room of them, please, over a whole dust of University professors, any day, starting now!

(You can keep the goggles.)

*R*arely Asked Questions:
How have you been affected by celebrity?

*W*HAT IS the stuff? What's celebrity?
What's fame? I so need definitions!

How have I been affected. How would you be affected, if you were me, someone calls a friend at a book-signing: "Ellen, you won't believe it!   I can't believe this!   It's Richard Bach!"

And Ellen looks at you, courteous but drawing a blank, "And you are . . . who?"

To one person, you're famous. To the person alongside you're so-what. How does that affect you?

A friend in the movie industry told me. "I was at a party, years ago, when Robert Redford walked into the room. Everything stopped. Never saw charisma like that. For a minute the room, and this is Hollywood; it went dead silent."

Yet earlier, when Redford was the struggling actor nobody heard of, where was the charisma, the celebrity, the fame? Missing, is where it was.

My guess—charisma comes as a light we shine on those we love. To stay charisma-free, stay unknown and unloved by others. Fame lies in someone else's perception of us, and even the most famous, I'll bet, still get their "And you are who?" moments.

I'm pretty sure I'm no celebrity; you've never seen a photo of me stepping on some red carpet.

I cannot tell if I'm famous. I sure don't feel that way . . . I'm a minor American writer, look for my name at the very bottom of the Sophisticated Literary Writers list.

Only those few who've been touched by a word I may have written which connects with the life they know, only that small faction of readers is even aware I exist. Of those who even remember a book's title, a tiny few recall the author's name.

I don't remember the titles of most of the books I read. Unless you've written a book that floored me, or a series of books that I think are terrific, you're who's-she, you're not famous to me.

Safest thing, I think, when your name's in the papers, is ever assume nobody's heard of you, and since that's mostly true, the attitude works well.

One nice thing about the craft of writing is that one can say what one needs to say and remain pretty well anonymous.

My picture is rarely on my book jackets, and then the publisher put it there without letting me know. My heart goes out to actors, poor lambs . . . when they're not recognized in public, their career is in trouble. Would you enjoy that life, to be recognized everywhere you go?

Once in the middle of a film project, I went grocery-shopping with the actor Cliff Robertson. He was surrounded by the time we hit the peanut-butter aisle, and graciously signed autographs while I snuck off and bought the groceries. Would I want that? Every day? Whuf!

My one taste of that sort of recognition happened the day after my picture was on the cover of Time magazine, sometime in the 70's. I was in Manhattan, walking to the office of the Macmillan Publishing Company, when someone in the crowd of pedestrians on 52nd Street looked at me (strange enough in Manhattan) and said, "You're Richard Bach!"

That kind of recognition, I've got to admit, is fun for a day or two. When you can't turn it off, though, week after month, it affects the way one lives one's life.

Affected me, for sure. It was way too much publicity, after Jonathan Seagull was published, and what happened is that I backed into shadows and have pretty well stayed there since. So what's a recluse doing with a website?

I love ideas, I guess, and the way they charge my life, take me off balance and then put me back. I love sharing the light of them with readers who care, same as I do. It may be that a website's one safe way to play with ideas and the few to whom they matter, and not get famous.

$\mathcal{L}$ucky and me

$\mathcal{H}$ERE'S THE LAST photo I took of my dog Lucky before he died.

We had been together ten years, nearly every day, or about 6,000 walks together. Sometimes he'd bark at things, he'd chase after rabbits to watch 'em run, bark at deer to see 'em run, go charging at me and away, get me to run, too.

He had a gait, a pace that was split-second rhythm, a furry steam-locomotive set to Long Distance Cruise: chuf-chuf-chuf-chuf-chuf . . . it was sheer beauty to watch that dog coming back to me after a rabbit-training session.

He'd get burrs in his fur, and stand patiently while I brushed them out, he'd lie on his observation-post at the hilltop by the house, looking over the island, checking all was peaceful in the valley below.

When we brought Zsa-Zsa home as a puppy, he looked at us. "A puppy. Are you sure you want to do this?"

When we said yes Lucky we're sure, he patiently withstood her needle-tooth attacks, taught her how to run really fast uphill and down, demonstrated his you-can-do-this-forever-and-not-get-tired locomotive pace, which ZZ never quite mastered.

I had always known that some day I'd have a dog named Lucky, and I guess he'd always known he'd have a man named Richard live with him for 50 dog-years or so. And thus begins my story.

With Lucky instantly dead, it was a test for my There's-No-Such-Thing-As-Dying conviction. Here's his body, unmoving, lifeless, and all at once a corner turned, I had a new connection with my dog.

"It's a hand-puppet, Richard! My body's a hand-puppet!"
It took me a minute to listen, to recognize this sudden new
voice in my mind was Lucky's, his spirit calling, helping me
understand.

"Remember Kermit the Frog? Kermit's body was a sock, it
was green terrycloth with shoe-button eyes and sewed-on
lashes!"

I remembered or maybe imagined backstage in-studio
Manhattan, there lay the world-famous Kermit the Frog,
tossed careless on a tabletop when filming was done. It was
a just a sock, unbreathing, unmoving. Cloth. Empty.

I blinked, and in my eyes again was Lucky's sock-puppet
body. No life there at all. "What made Kermit live?"

Well, sure, a puppet's life is the spirit of its puppeteer. Jim
Henson's soul filled his empty puppet on a stage that could
not contain Jim Henson himself, not without shattering the
illusion of Kermit as a separate actor, Kermit observing the
world, Kermit dancing, singing, playing a frog-guitar on that
lily-pad in his home swamp:
Why are there so many/
Songs about rainbows,/
And what's on the other side?

"Richard, when I decided to withdraw my spirit, which you
cannot see with your eyes, you are left with my sock-puppet
body, which you can. You shed your tears over terrycloth
fur while I run happy and free in Light! Would you cry this
moment if you had senses that would show me with you? If
you could see me now, filled with perfect life, would you still
grieve?"

That was the change in our friendship, Lucky's and mine. He was no longer my dog, he was . . . .

A week later, I talked with an animal communicator in Seattle, Debbie Vaughn. She got in touch with Lucky the spirit, and after telling me some things about him which she could not otherwise have known, she was open for questions.

"What was it like, Lucky?," I asked, "what was it like to die?"

"There was the shock," Deborah said, listening. "But after the shock there was no pain, and I was held in a beautiful Warmth."

"And then I got bigger. Bigger and bigger, I was expanding out into the stars and I was omnipotent, I was everything!"

In the course of an hour's talk, Deborah/Lucky didn't mention a word about grief or sorrow. "He's like a scientist," she told me. "He's just utterly rational."

That's one way I'd describe my dog, too: Lucky the cool detached observer of the world around him, the way he watched the valley from his special spot on the ridge.

"I am always with you. I am the trees of the forest, I am the air you breathe."

Why these tears as I write, when I know that being ever with those we love is nothing sad at all?

That's when I realized some facts had changed. Lucky was no longer my dog, he had let go, at least for a while, his attachment to form. Gone the form of a Shetland Sheepdog, all chestnut and black and white-ruff ascot and gloves; gone those dark dark eyes that watched and smiled and said, "Don't you know who I am?"

Lucky had become teacher for me; Lucky knew more about the world of spirit than I did, and I yearned to understand. He could never have taught me so long as he stood fifteen inches high at the shoulder. Now, encompassing the universe, he can.

Spirit does not require body to exist, any more than Jim Henson required a hand-puppet to be who he is. Spirit requires form, it needs a body only when it chooses to act on a stage where bodies are our costumes.

A month later I talked with Patty Summers, an animal communicator three thousand miles east.

I asked the same questions I had asked Debbie Vaughn. Patty did the same thing, described Lucky before she spoke for him. "He's very gentle, a gentleness about him. Extremely sweet, easy. There's a politeness about him. If Lucky were a person, he would have dressed nicely, well-mannered.

"The first thing that hits me is this gentle warmth. As if you're sitting on the lounge chair in a perfect spring or fall day not too warm not too cold, a quiet peaceful loving warmth. He's sitting there with this smile on his face.

"All of a sudden he feels like he's expanding out, like he's touching everything, expanding and expanding and expanding, becoming a part of everything. Some sensation of seeing other beings, other dogs and humans, not much, he moves past that quickly. I just feel connected to every . . . everything."

Different words, Patty used, but the same pictures I had heard before. And not a word about concern for grief or sorrow, as though such things were beneath mention from Lucky's view, as though they were infinitely unimportant.

"I'm supposed to tell you he had a spot outside where he would just want to lay there and observe, like a lookout. To tell you sometime you can see him there. It's not your imagination—if you haven't seen him, you will."

Aren't the truths we learn sometimes wildly fascinating, at the same time there's this little smile-of-the-universe about them? My dog has become my spiritual master, the guide at whose paws I've already taken a great step forward, understanding who I am.

I still have dogs at home. Well, I used to think of them as dogs.

There's Zsa-Zsa, for instance. Do I salute her, awe and respect for her own spirit, bigger than the universe?

Look now. She's pretending to be a dog. She wants us to believe she's not Infinite Spirit true as us, she's just a little doggie with a stick . . .

*A*utographology

I USED TO WONDER about autographs.

What is so important, what is the compelling magnetism in someone's signature of their own name? Everybody has their own way of writing, of course they do, but what difference does it make, how we trace our letters?

Every once in a while I'd find a signed copy of a book, glance at the inscription: Jane Johnson. Or Best Wishes, Jane Johnson.

Why would anybody cherish a copy of a book because someone had . . . well, because they had wrecked the thing by writing in it?

Then for a while, I don't know why maybe because my higher self got tired of hearing me whining about why autographs, I wondered on graphology. Do we really scroll our inner character along with the characters we write by hand?

Not hardly, I thought, but I'll read whatever you have to say of what you've learned, Mr. Handwriting Expert.

I finished the book, changed. Why, It does have meaning, after all, those lines we make on paper!

I tried it on myself, laughing. I couldn't escape! Unless I faked shamelessly, writing left-handed on the lid of a half-gallon can in the paint-shaker, I sketched my own portrait in the way I wrote.

Didn't matter what words. The quick brown fox jumps over the lazy dog will do just fine, thank you.

"Ah," said my inner graphoanalyst. "Note the instrument he uses to write . . . a felt-tip calligraphic pen, in black ink."

Of course, I thought. I like that pen.

The analyst, he fixed me with a piercing gaze. "Could have chosen a pencil why not! Could have picked the ball-point, or the crayon, or the charcoal, or the fountain-pen or the bamboo ink-brush, could have chosen fine-tip or medium or extra-broad, the hard graphite or the soft, the square-section or rectangular or octagon or round. Could have chosen the feather-quill I had laid out on the table before you why no other but the felt-tip. Why the felt-tip medium-wide calligraphic in black?"

I felt the eyes boring into me even though I was using them to look at my pen.

I swallowed, nervous. "Because I like it?"

A-HA! Please note that he likes that particular pen and no other and this in itself is deep insight into who this man may be, before ever he has uncapped his precious stylus.

"You will write for me, now, please. The quick brown fox . . ."

"I already wrote for you. The whole first chapter of Illusions is my handwriting."

"You will write for me, now, please. The quick brown fox . . ."

I did as I was told, over and again, to fill the page.

"And sign it, please, when you are finished."

I signed.

A long silence, inspecting the page. Technical murmurs from my own expert within.

"Mmmm. Lines slant upward . . . an optimist, are we? No dots over the 'I's' – we don't much care for details, do we?"

On it went, at quite some length: the arch personal comments he had for the height of my ascenders, depth of my descenders, my average slant, space on the left, space on the right, margin variations, letter-space, word-space, punctuation anomalies, print-to-cursive ratio, readability variation in text, intensity of error-correction, original letter-constructs, initial capital first name signature, initial capital last name, signature readability, changing pressures on the stylus . . .

The humming stopped. A long silence. "Yes," I said to me, "We are certainly you!"

Then the analyst said that he was hungry, could we have a grilled cheese sandwich. Not another word about handwriting.

Now he's gone off to study edible wild plants, his current obsession. I lag behind, enjoying the shards of what he learned about handwriting.

I found a photograph of an original signed copy of Antoine de Saint-Exupery's *Wind, Sand and Stars*. Saint-Ex was a tall man, but here this small neat hand, carefully spelling his name on a dead-straight line, the letters original, almost code-for-letters. He cared for detail in an absent-minded way (note the dot sailing way over the "i"), he had no grand feelings of superiority, was a servant to his ideas.

Look at Ray Bradbury's signature in a copy of *The Illustrated Man*. Talk about bold! The terminal "Y" sweeping back to underline the name, and drawings and colors and exclamation points!

Sure of himself, trusting his vision, untouched by doubt.

Since all this educating, I understand about autographs. In fact, should you need to know the secret of my being, attached is the page I wrote by hand, about a fox named Lightning and his dog, Drowsy.

Both of them?

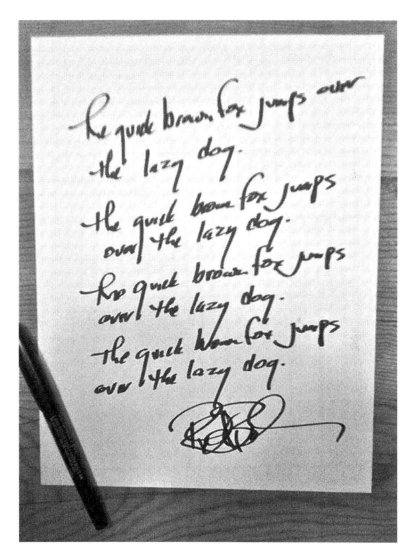

*F*ams

*I*F SOMEONE we believe is famous, let's say the American actor George Clooney, really likes the work of someone else we think is famous, let's say the Italian actress Sophia Loren, and she in turn really likes George Clooney's films, who's the fan?

When they meet, knowing this, do they treat each other as fans?

I know this sounds silly, but there's a point to my little thought-experiment, and it turns around the word "fan."

So far as I know, the word comes, after pausing in Latin for "temple," from "Fanatic: A person marked or motivated by an extreme, unreasoning enthusiasm, a person whose enthusiasm or zeal for something is extreme or beyond normal limits."

When you're in the vicinity of a person thus described, do you feel a little ill-at-ease? Almost as if the person might suddenly say or do something extreme or unreasoning or beyond normal limits and shatter your otherwise pleasant day and that of others around you?

Yet, neither Ms. Loren nor Mr. Clooney would likely do any such shattering, should they meet. They may appreciate each other's work, be glad for each other's very existence, yet still enjoy a gentle happy conversation that leaves them both delighted that they've met. How can this be?

Here's how: they may be fans, but each already respects the other.

So if celebrities can be each others' fans of the gentle kind, why do the rest of us have to worry about extreme unreasoning enthusiasm, when we find that we're meeting someone who likes our work?

We don't, if: If we slide the last letter of "fan" one notch toward the beginning of the alphabet, if we change "fan for fanatic" to "fam for family" all of a sudden we've got a meeting between those of shared values, those who know that respect for each other goes both ways.

And so what?

For the last forty years, on and off, I've met many readers

of my books. In bookstores, at airports, at talks I've given and appearances I've made, I've never met one soul who shattered my day with extreme behavior.

Sometimes there are tears, so glad can we be to find another who shares our ideals; more often hugs and handshakes . . . we meet at last! These are touching events, you can feel the respect of everyone for another.

In the days when there used to be long lines at bookstore au-tographings, some would become good friends simply talk-ing together as they waited, the line creeping forward since it takes longer to do my artwork on a title page than just to sign my name.

The only shatterings I've had, have come from those few who decided on their own to seek me out not at some family event but one-on-one no notice no warning.

Perhaps three individuals stalked me for a while over the years, while another thought I needed to be killed. Those, may have been fans.

Fams, you can bet: we get along just fine.

Rarely Asked Questions:
  "What aircraft have you flown?"

HERE'S HAPPY remembering!

Technically, I guess you're asking which types of aircraft I've flown as pilot in command. So I won't count the F-106 flight in which I was a back-seater through Mach 2. Believe it or not, a tame flight.

We hit that speed at 42,000 feet, so looking down over the ocean, it felt as if we were crawling along. Only the needle of the machmeter showing "2.02 said we were moving twice the speed of sound.

On the other hand I'll note that the Piper Cub, door open at 75 mph, blurring ten feet above summer hayfields, is going like a rocket.

The first airplane in which I was a passenger was a Globe Swift, a GC-1B in 1951. So I must have been fifteen years old. I didn't start flight training till 1954.

Here's the list (the asterisks are the 35 airplane types I've owned):

US Air Force:
Beech T-34A, North American T-28A, Lockheed T-33A, North American F-86F, F-86H, Republic F-84F, North American F-100F, Douglas C-47, Fairchild C-123, Fairchild C-119G and C-119J.

Civilian aircraft (including some WWI military replicas): Luscombe 8E, Luscombe 8A, *Piper J-3 Cub, *Piper J-3S (on floats), Aeronca 12AC Chief (on wheels and skis), *Aeronca 7AC Champ, Aeronca Sedan (on wheels and floats), Taylorcraft BC-12D (wheels and floats), Piper Tripacer, Piper Colt, Piper PA-18 Super Cub, Snow AG-2, Grumman Ag-Cat, Call-Air, Auster, *DH-82 Tiger Moth, *DH-89 Dragon Rapide, *North American P-51D, *BD-5J, *Grumman G-44 Widgeon, *Aviat Husky A-1B, *Cessna 310 Riley Rocket, *Lake Buccaneer, Lake Renegade, *Beech T-34B, *Lockheed T-33A, *Pterodactyl Ascender (built it from a kit), *Quicksilver Sport IIS, Stampe SV-4, *Parks P-2A, *Globe Swift GC-1B, *Republic RC-3 Seabee, *Pitts S-2A, *Pitts S-1, DH Gipsy Moth, Fokker D-VII, Pfalz D-III, SE-5A, Currie Wot SE-5, Caudron 277, Luciole, Beech Bonanza, Travel Air 2000, *Travel Air 4000, Great Lakes 2T-1A, *Consolidated Fleet II, *Meyers 200D, Cessna 337 Skymaster, *Cessna P337 Pressurized Skymaster, Hughes 269B, *Hughes 300C, *Hiller 12E, Hiller FH-1100, Schweizer 1-26 sailplane, Schweizer 1-23, Schweizer 2-33, Schweizer 1-35, *Schleicher ASW-15, *Schleicher ASW-17, *Lark IL-28 motorglider, *Wills

Wing 125 Paraglider, Mooney Mk 20, Waco UPF-7, Stearman PT-17, Stinson Jr. S, Buecker Jungmann, Cessna 120, Cessna 140, Cessna 150, Cessna 152, Cessna 172, Cessna 175, Cessna 180, Cessna 182, Cessna 206, Cessna 210, Cessna 320A, Cessna Airmaster, Jodel 150, Bellanca 200, Bellanca 260, Stinson Voyager, Piper Comanche, Piper Twin Comanche, UC-1 Twin Bee, North American SNJ-5, *Reed Clip-Wing Cub, Fairchild PT-13, Fairchild PT-19, *Fairchild 24R, *Ryan PT-22, Piper Cherokee 160, Citabria, *SFS-31 motorglider, *Fournier RF-4, TF-51 Cavalier, Aero Commander 560F, Beech Bellanca 300, Piper PA-22 (on floats), Bellanca Champ, Helio Courier, Bolkow Junior, Blanik, Pratt-Read, RANS S-6, *B1-RD, *Grumman Cheetah, Grumman Traveler, Waco 220, Mooney Mark 21, American Yankee, Alon Aircoupe, and 51 sky-diving jumps in some kind of square parachute which type having been nearly killed in it I don't recall.

*I*f This Story is Political, I'm Takin' it Down.

YOU'D THINK the New York Times and I would be great friends.

The newspaper published a little story I wrote long ago about managing to win a game from a highly touted chess computer. (IBM claimed that it was a computer error that allowed a mistake and would I please go away and not come back.)

Then the Times sent me a news item, that Jonathan Seagull had been declared an enemy of the Chinese people (along with Beethoven, as I recall), and did I care to comment.

I did care to comment, and my demand for satisfaction from Premier Zhou Enlai, that we resolve the issue through a winner-take-all table tennis match between him and me was issued on the pages of that newspaper.

I may have inferred that I possessed skill and speed in serves and returns somewhat in excess of the truth, but no matter, my challenge was sufficiently ferocious that the Premier did not respond, and I consider myself victor by default.

Over the years, five of my books have been on the Times' Best-Seller List, a couple or three for more than a year running. You'd think the Times and me were old pals.

Yet a few weeks ago I wrote a piece for the Op-Ed section of that paper. Sent it to them by high-speed priority email, no less. But what to my wondering eyes would appear was not a miniature sleigh, but . . . nothing. No answer. No response whatever, although the site guaranteed an acknowledgement in two days, or three, or some very short time.

After a week, not a word. So of course I sent the story again, with a header requesting that a human being scan the text, instead of a machine.

Zippo.

A third time I sent the story, and a third time . . . utter silence.

Now I am not sophisticated when it comes to politics and it occurred to me that this was the Times' gentle way of telling old friends that they are not politically in tune with the requirements of the newspaper.

I'm not kidding—to this day I don't know whether my little story offended the editor or not.

Here's what I wrote, not for flyers but for a general reader. And honest, would somebody please tell me of course the Times couldn't print my story and that all of sudden I've gone political without knowing it? Apologies in advance, etc, etc, if I come off as a clueless boffin:

WAR WITH IRAN?

Look, I know the arguments:
General Electric and Lockheed-Martin earn a couple dollars on hardware;
We get a drop or two of oil;
Three guys at the top quit calling us The Great Satan, at last.

But go to war with a whole country, war with Iran for the sake of two drops, two dollars and silence? Somebody in the last couple administrations must have had their hat on backwards.

Remember Iran before the revolution? Remember they called Tehran the Paris of the East, with lovely women and handsome guys all dancing of an eve, their perfect fashions on their spotless boulevards?

Remember their smile, the class and flash with which they were trippin' down the streets of the city, callin' a name that's lighter than air?

These are beautiful people.

Sure enough, some fuzzies came along and promised to kill them if they didn't wear blankets instead of Saint Laurent. They chafed for a time and then they rose up and nearly took their country back, nearly won the right to be free again.

These are courageous people.

This next part may seem a bit parochial to you, but listen up, pretend you're me, it's the whole point of this story:

I've got readers in Iran.

There's a raft of Iranians who've read and liked my books, same as some Americans have read and liked them. You're right, I haven't had any Ayatollah fan mail, but to be fair I haven't had any American-presidential fan mail, either. And that's fine by me.

Books aren't written for everyone, but for a family of readers to whom they make sense and bring an evening's pleasure.

I don't mind the Commander-in-Chief deciding we need to

kill most of the population of this foreign country or that one, as there is a certain charm in killing folks and taking their stuff, but excuse me I'd like to draw a line when it comes to offing my readers.

All due respect, these folks happen to be my livelihood. Hello America? Do you have any idea what happens to your writers when you kill their readers?

You don't know I'll tell you: we starve. Maybe not starve, but we have to put off buying that neat little airplane we've wanted for weeks now, and it's no fun being a writer when your Commander-in-Chief takes it to mind he needs to destroy the folks who buy your stories.

I can't count how many sales I've lost in Iraq, in Afghanistan, now in Yemen and Libya and Pakistan. I've got several thousand readers in Syria and here comes this creepy feeling I'll be losing them too, right soon.

I'm no diplomatic expert and don't get me wrong—if we have to shoot men and women to save them from their cruel government, shoot we must.

I'm telling you hey not Iran, d'you hear? Because what happens when the C-in-C kills them is that I have to sell an airplane to survive, and airplanes in case you haven't checked our economy are not exactly gold mines for sellers.

What happens after we incinerate Iran at no cost to our country or to our joy of living?

Here's what happens: my readers are gone. I'm on the street, me and Stephen King and Tom Clancy and Danielle Steele . . .

we've been years gathering our families of readers around the world and let me tell you none of us are terribly happy with the familycide that's been going on this last decade or so.

Our books are published in Farsi, all through the Middle East, in Hebrew and Turkish and Greek and Russian, in Hindi and Thai and Chinese, not to mention in languages with readers not drawn up just yet in a Contingency Attack Plan.

Do you know who pays our bills, do you know who supports Danny and Steve and Tom and me when our readers and their bookstores and their libraries are blown to shreds with missiles and cluster-bombs and drones and hand grenades?

You do, dear reader. Steve and Tom and Danny and me are on the dole, instead of pens in our hands, it's palms-up to the U.S. government, namely you, to keep us alive don't even talk about in any condition to write for our non-existent families.

I'll be chatting with my colleagues this week, and my guess is they'll join me in an offer to the President: we shall promise personally to pay for the oil-drops and couple-bucks of mil-spec hardware, in return for a guarantee to leave our Iranian readers alive at least until after we've finished writing stories and retire to Aspen or Palm Springs or Sanibel Island.

We all love a country, don't we, that's savvy enough not to blow away its own markets? I'll tell you I do.

God bless America!

—Richard Bach

—end of NY Times story—

414

So. If you find this story to be offensive or political . . . well, this isn't a political site and out she goes if anybody objects. Maybe it's the hat on backwards line. Is that too aggressive? I didn't mean it, like, literally.

$\mathcal{L}$ife in the Afterworld

$\mathcal{W}$E CAN LEARN A LOT about the world that follows after we're done living in this one. Just reading, and we'll know. And talking with others and then putting things together, one after another.

There used to be a problem for me with heaven. They said that animals come to visit us there, or maybe they just live in quiet places where the frogs and raccoons live, where there are little rivers and quiet ponds where they can relax after a difficult lifetime on earth.

But deers and antelopes, I thought, they're tired of being dinners after a while, for the lions and tigers and hyenas. And of course for being targets the humans around here, that enjoy shooting animals for sport. Once you've lived with the animals in a forest, you get to know them. Day after day. They'll sleep in the meadow, once they know you're not out of shoot them, and when your dog learns to be friends and play with them.

Live a life here, be a kind human to the deer (and antelopes, in other places), and you realize they have a right to live here, too, just like us. It goes on through the seasons, in the winters when we can put little things for them to snack on.

Begin a life with them like this, and all of a sudden you can be distressed by some guy you've never seen before, walking on your land, and the deers land, in a camouflage suit and a rifle. He intends to kill a deer!

He doesn't know about their personalities or their sense of humor, he doesn't know that you've named them and they come to you for a little treat in the middle of the snows. He doesn't know that Gina has two little ones, Elektra and Bambi, following her around after they're born; that she teaches them how to travel, where to sleep, what to be careful about some wild foods, and others that are delicious.

Just this stranger, who wants to change their astonishing grace into an unmoving, a dead body. Where do her fawns go, how to they learn when their mom has been killed?

Hunters might say, "It happens in heaven, too, I'm sure. Do you want the lions go hungry, the tigers losing weight, and the hunters there, well not having fun, killing things? Do you know that raccoons kill frogs, by the way? Everything is built to eat something else. Even us. Unless you're a vegetarian, and there are not many of those. Do you want some meat, by the way? I don't eat my targets."

For a long time, I didn't have an answer for them. I just put NO HUNTING signs around me, till the place had enough homes near that most hunters didn't come here again. Thoughtful for humans, but not quite so caring for deer.

Then I read some more from those who had spent a few minutes or an hour or so in the afterworld, the near-death experiencers.

"What a beautiful place, heaven is! Why you can travel from anywhere at the speed of thought, you have crystal cities, if you like city life, and lands without end with trees and lakes and animals. And of course, you're never hungry! You're a spirit, so you don't need food, though you can imagine some, if you feel like it. Thoughtforms. Everything there is a thoughtform."

And I said, "Well that's nice, but what about lions?"

They considered that I hadn't heard a word they had said. "Lions don't get hungry, either, Richard."

"Raccoons?"

"No, raccoons don't get hungry. And frogs don't get hungry, and cows and deer don't get hungry. Nobody gets hungry." And then a gentle question for me, "Do you know what a thoughtform is?"

I knew. "Thank you for telling me what you found," I said, "and thank you for remembering, when your body was nearly dead, and thanks for coming back to earth and telling us what you saw."

Sure enough, deer and lions have things to learn here on earth, just the same as we do. But there may be a time when all of a sudden we don't much care for meat, any more. As far as I can tell, little Bambi has not had a near-death experience, but I sense that he likes the idea of lions not killing deer, and not being hungry, either.

Lions are away over the sea, most of them, but could our own hunters consider that idea, too? There's money to be made in target shooting, and in teaching self-defense. It isn't lions that are predators for us, these days, there are humans who do that.

In case they love guns (like I do) but choose a different target and a slight change of mind about hunting, Bambi sends us his warm regards, direct from his own forest, on earth, here and now.

*R*emembering the Messiah's Handbook

*T*HE LAST TIME I SAW the *Messiah's Handbook* was when I threw it away.

I had been using it as I was taught in Illusions: hold question in mind, close eyes, open handbook at random, pick left page or right. Eyes open, read answer.

Always before it worked: fear dissolved in a smile, doubt lifted by sudden understanding. Always had I been charmed and entertained by what these pages had to tell me.

So that dark day I opened the book, trusting. "Why did my friend Donald Shimoda, who had so much to teach that we so needed to learn, why did he have to die such a senseless death?"

Eyes open, listen to the answer:

Everything in this book may be wrong.

A burst of night and rage, I remember, instant fury. I turn to it for help and *this is my answer?* I threw the book as hard and as far from me as I could, pages fluttering above that nameless Iowa hayfield, the thing tumbling in slow motion, shuddering forever down toward the weeds. I didn't watch to see where it fell.

I flew from that field and never flew back. The handbook, that senseless hurtful agony-page, was gone.

Twenty years later came a package to a writer in care of the publisher. In the package a note:

Dear Richard Bach, I found this when I was plowing my dad's soybean field. The field's a quarter-section used to be in hay and he told me you landed there once with the guy they killed they said was magic. So this has been plowed under I guess for a long time else it's been disked and harrowed every year and nobody's seen it till now. For all that, it's not much hurt and I figured it's your property and if you're still alive you ought to have it.

No return address. On the pages, my own fingerprints in engine oil from an old Fleet biplane, a sifting of coarse dusts, a stem or two of grass falling out when I fanned it open.

Rage gone, I held the book a long time, remembering.

Everything in this book may be wrong. Sure enough. But

everything may be right, as well. Right and wrong's not up to a book. I'm the only one to say what's true for me. I'm responsible.

I leafed through the pages, wondering. Is the book returned to me the same one I threw away, so long ago? Had it been resting quietly underground or had it been changing to become what some future reader needed to remember?

At last, eyes closed, I held the handbook once more and asked.

Dear strange mystical volume, why did you come back? Riffled the pages for a moment, opened my eyes and saw.

Every person,
all the events of your life,
are there because you have drawn them there.

What you choose to do with them
is up to you.

I smiled, reading that. And I chose, this time, instead of throwing it away, to keep the *Messiah's Handbook.*

And I choose now, instead of wrapping it in silence, to let you unwrap the whole of it and listen to its whisper for yourself, whenever you wish.

Some of the ideas I've found in this book I've said in others: There are words here from *Illusions* and *One* and *Jonathan Livingston Seagull* and *Out of My Mind* and *The Ferret Chronicles.* A writer's life, like a reader's, is fiction and fact; it's almost-happened and half-remembered and once-dreamed. The smallest part of our being is history that somebody else can verify.

Yet fiction and truth are friends; the only way to tell some truths is in the language of stories.

Donald Shimoda, for instance, my reluctant Messiah, is a real person, though as far as I know he's never had a mortal body or a voice that anyone else could hear. So is Stormy Ferret real, flying her miniature transport through a terrible storm because she believes in her mission; so is Harley Ferret throwing himself into a midnight sea to save his friend; so are all these characters real who have brought me to life.

Enough explaining. Before you may take a handbook home, however, test this copy, be sure it works.

Hold a question in mind, please. Now close your eyes, open the handbook at random and pick left page or right,

—Richard Bach

Books by Richard Bach

Stranger to the Ground
Biplane
Nothing by Chance
Jonathan Livingston Seagull
A Gift of Wings
Illusions: The Adventures of a Reluctant Messiah
There's No Such Place as Far Away
The Bridge Across Forever
One
Running from Safety
Out of My Mind
Messiah's Handbook
Hypnotizing Maria
Rescue Ferrets at Sea
Air Ferrets Aloft
Rancher Ferrets on the Range
Writer Ferrets: Chasing the Muse
The Last War: Detective Ferrets & the Golden Deed
Curious Lives: Adventures from the Ferret Chronicles
Thank Your Wicked Parents
Travels with Puff: A Gentle Game of Life and Death
Illusions II: The Adventures of a Reluctant Student
Part-Time Angels